RUFUS REMEMBERS

For: John.
with best wishes
from
[signature]
30.7.98

RUFUS REMEMBERS

*The Autobiography
of
Rufus Heald* MBE

JANUS PUBLISHING COMPANY
London, England

First published in Great Britain 1997
by Janus Publishing Company
Edinburgh House, 19 Nassau Street
London W1N 7RE

Copyright © Rufus Heald 1997

British Library Cataloguing-in-Publication Data.
A catalogue record for this book is available from the British Library.

ISBN 1 85756 381 6

Cover design Harold King

Photoset by Keyboard Services, Luton
Printed and bound in England by
Antony Rowe Ltd, Chippenham, Wilts

Contents

The author in London, 1948

1

Early Days: 1925–47

I was born in London in 1925, and the whole of the population of France went out celebrating that day. I think this was probably due to the fact that it was also Bastille Day rather than the fact that it was my birthday, but nevertheless it was nice of them all to celebrate such an important day. I have promised myself that I will celebrate the occasion in France one year.

I understand that I was the first of a pair of twins. My brother did not survive but the psychologists would say that this has given me my sense of competitiveness and a determination to always be part of the winning team. I wouldn't know if that is true or not, I'm too close to the trees to see the wood, but it is very true that I am a bad loser and I hate anyone to do better than me. This, of course shows up in the way I drive my cars. Always high-performance vehicles and always driven fairly hard and with a good measure of aggression. This has not resulted in a bad accident record so it seems that I keep it under control – just (or else I have just been lucky). As is usual, I have little recollection of those very early days but I do remember that I used to get involved in 'disagreements' with my sister. Since she was fourteen months older than me, she usually won. I also remember that for a number of years when other children whom I knew were having a party, several of the guests, when invited, used to ask: 'Is Rufus going to be there?' If the reply was 'Yes' then they almost invariably said: 'Oh good, that means that there will be a fight!' It seems that I got embroiled in fights more often than not and frequently had to be taken home in disgrace.

My only other claims to fame are that shortly after being born, I was christened at a very smart church in central London. I should have been the main attraction but my godfathers rather stole the show. The first one was His Royal Highness the Prince Arthur, Duke of Connaught, and the second was Sir Stafford Cripps QC, the famous barrister at law. He was chosen because my father and he were in chambers together and the Prince because he was a friend of my maternal grandmother, the Lady Angela St Clair Erskine. She herself first achieved fame, or notoriety depending on your point of view, when she opened a canteen, called Angela's, for the troops in France during the First World War. For those readers who have seen the film *The Monocled Mutineer*, the actress who played her part was very like her to look at.

In the fullness of time, I was sent to a series of boarding schools, most of which failed dismally in their efforts to educate and civilise me, but I ended up at Wellington College in Berkshire. Here I seemed to fit in to some extent – or maybe I was getting bored with being a rebel – and they not only managed to teach me a little, but they also introduced me to military-type discipline. The 1939 War intervened in my education and true to form, having been at an army-orientated school, I volunteered for the Royal Air Force, even if for no other reason than that my father was in the RAF. My primary hope was to be accepted for pilot training and, after a prolonged period of tests and assessments, I eventually persuaded the Air Force that I was suitable material to be trained as a pilot.

Early Days: 1925–47

Schooldays

In the meantime ... my academic career was not an out-standing one but I thoroughly enjoyed Mathematics, Physics and Chemistry. Wellington had some excellent teachers of these subjects and they encouraged me, with a modicum of success. When the time came to take my School Certificate Examinations, I managed to get Distinctions or Credits in all four of the science subjects. Although they were normally taken as two subjects, Mathematics, and Physics and Chemistry, I was advised to take them as four separate subjects, Basic Mathematics, Additional Mathematics, Physics, and Chemistry. I found this particularly valuable several years later when I took specialised further training in Pure Mathematics, Applied Mathematics, Physics and Chemistry. I'm sure that a high proportion of what I was taught in those distant days has leaked through the sieve by now, but I still have a love of numbers and can work aviation-related calculations out in my head, quicker than I can with a computer.

I was also forced to take up sport at Wellington. Cricket left me cold so, in the summer, I was a member of the athletics squad – I used to run the half-mile – and in the winter I played both rugby and hockey. I have found over the years that a lot of people seem to think that hockey is a bit of a game for softies. Well, rugby is thought of as a hard game but it has a relatively large, soft ball which is thrown about or kicked. In hockey we have a small, very hard ball and we are armed with a stick or club. I have come off the hockey pitch after a match, with blood running off me in several places and numerous lumps, far more often than I have come off the rugby pitch with anything worse than a bruise and a winding. A slim guy like me can get a bit squashed in the middle of a scrum or maul, but I should not have been there anyhow as I usually played as a wing three-quarter. I abandoned the athletics and rugby after I joined the RAF but I carried on with my hockey and played for

3

various RAF and civilian teams over the years. I never did get much of a kick out of watching matches. It was a case of 'compete (and win), or find something else to do'. In sport, as in many things, I have always taken the view that I am there to win. I have freely admitted that I am a bad loser, but whatever I have done either on the sports field or at work, it has always been my aim to do it really well – and better than the other guys around me. This has made me a few enemies over the years, but that's life. Later into my career, I took up sailing and badminton. The former because it looked like fun and because it has a lot of similarity with aviation, and the latter because it is a very fast game and gave me an evening activity. But as with other sports, whenever I sailed I was trying very hard to win every race I entered. No way was I there 'just to make up the numbers'. I even succeeded in winning a few.

Join Up

In 1942, I was attested into the RAF but due to the backlog of aircrew training I was put on deferred service for a while. Initially I went to the Bristol Aeroplane Company's Apprentice School at Filton, near Bristol, and there I was given the rudiments of skill both with hand and machine tools. From here, I went to work with a company called Nash & Thompson just outside Surbiton on the Kingston by-pass. This company used to make Frazer Nash motor cars before the war but now they were part of the Development Division of Parnell Aircraft. I was working in the electrical research section where new, electrically operated gun turrets were being designed and tested. The company as a whole manufactured the Frazer-Nash gun turrets for Lancasters, Wellingtons, Whitleys and Halifax aircraft and, when I joined them, they were working on the design of an electrically driven mid-upper turret for the Lincoln bomber and a new, electrically operated tail turret for the Lancaster. As you will realise this was a fascinating place to work and also

4

some of the knowledge of machine guns and aircraft cannon came in useful to me when I was ordered to report for my pilot training. But that's another story. In the meanwhile, my 'big sister' had joined the ATS where she seemed to have enjoyed herself and indeed she entered the history books when she typed out the original English version of the Surrender Document signed by the Germans in the field. (The original has her initials 'S N H' on the back in pencil.) My father was also in the RAF during the whole of the war: he had a variety of staff jobs usually in 'air intelligence', ending up on Lord Tedder's staff at Supreme Headquarters Allied Forces Europe (Lord Tedder was General Eisenhower's deputy at Supreme Headquarters Allied Forces in Europe.)

The Air Crew Reception Centre at Regent's Park in London was the Mecca to which the many thousand aircrew recruits were sent for their basic introduction into the Royal Air Force. The first thing the Air Force did, was to issue us with all our kit and for this we were marched off to Lord's Cricket Ground. I have never been there before or after, but in those days it was a most intimidating place. Vast queues of guys waiting for everything under the sun. The kit issue was the main point of the procedure, but we spent endless hours filling in forms and visiting doctors and dentists who ensured that we were all healthy enough to start training. I didn't see anyone fail the medical but perhaps the doctors reckoned that the training would get us fit? Anyhow we collected the usual stack of badly made, ill fitting uniforms and returned to Viceroy Court on the edge of Regent's Park where we were billeted. This was a block of flats which had been gutted and restocked with beds and not much else. We normally lived about eight to a room – a small room, in four two-tier bunks. Every day all our kit had to be laid out on display on the bed, and everything had to be positioned just so. Many a guy ended up with extra duties for having his plimsolls laced up the wrong way or for some other heinous crime of similar importance. No doubt it was good for our souls but we certainly didn't think so at the time. Many an hour was spent on drill, physical exercise, route marches and kit inspections.

After a short period we were paraded early one morning with all our kit on our shoulders and marched to the station. Here we were pushed into a train in which there were several reserved carriages – with seating for about 60 per cent of us and some many hours later we were let out on to another station. This turned out to be Torquay but not for us the joys of the South Devonshire seaside. We were chivvied from pillar to post and just as we were at last getting sorted out, the powers that be decided to move us to Babbacombe. This is another seaside town just north of Torquay. As usual in the Services in those days we were expected to march the several miles over the hills with all our kit on our shoulders. I don't know about the others but I was sagging at the knees when we eventually arrived. We spent several months there completing our Initial Training. This consisted of all the usual drill manoeuvres, plenty of route marches, lots of PT, frequent classroom lectures on subjects related to aviation and on the whole we had a pretty good time. It looks better in retrospect than it did at the time but so do many experiences.

From Babbacombe, we were split up into smaller groups and I and some others were sent to a small airfield called Clyffe Pypard, in Wiltshire. Here we joined a larger group for our initial Flying Grading because it was here that they decided who was a potential pilot, who was a potential navigator and who was a potential air gunner – and who was neither. While I was learning to fly the Tiger Moth, I was lucky enough to witness a remarkable accident. The only injury was to a pilot's pride and on the whole that was a self-inflicted injury.

We did our flying at a small grass airfield called RAF Alton Barnes 'somewhere in southern England' and one day a very smart Piper Cub arrived on the airfield, flown by an overseas pilot whose uniform was the smartest thing we has ever seen. He had three rows of medals, so was obviously a very experienced aviator and yet he was only two or three years older than we were. I guess he was about 21 or 22. Having patronised us for about half an hour, and after a mug of NAAFI tea, he went to his aircraft with the intention of flying back to his own base. He went to the cockpit, and turned various bits on. He then walked to the port side of the engine and proceeded to swing the propeller while standing facing forward, just in front of the port strut. Nothing happened. He reset some of the controls and tried again. We all stood there watching. After about a dozen fruitless swings, the engine at last caught and burst into life. Not just into life but into a pretty full-blooded roar. The aircraft started to roll forward (that's right, the brakes were either ineffective or not on, and no, he didn't bother with chocks). Anyhow the engine did its stuff and the aircraft started to move forward with increasing speed, while the pilot tried to duck under the strut to get to the door to do something to stop it. That's right – as you have probably guessed, he finally fell over in the soft English mud. Undeterred, he leapt to his feet and sprinted after his aircraft. He even managed to catch up with it. Well, he caught up with the tail and he was still gripping the rudder when the assembly reached the boundary of our not very big airfield. And stopped suddenly. Undeterred, the pilot over ran the tail, put his foot through the tailplane in so doing, and again fell flat on his face – in more ways than one. We were very impressed. I don't need to point out all the many things which the pilot either did and shouldn't have done; nor do I need to point out the things which he should not have done – but did. It's great fun pointing the finger of scorn at someone else but just remember, there but for the grace of God . . .

Having completed some eight hours' flying in Tiger Moths, including some solo circuits, we considered that we were pretty good pilots and we all looked forward to being posted to a Spitfire Squadron. Silly us! Military services don't work like that. At the end of the grading school, we were all returned to A.C.R.C. at Regent's Park for additional aptitude tests. So once more we had to try and convince the RAF that we were definitely fighter pilot material. In fact they didn't discriminate between fighter pilots and bomber pilots at that stage, so we were wasting our efforts. I was one of the lucky ones and again I was selected for pilot training rather than training for one of the other air-crew trades: navigator, bomb aimer or air gunner. Having finally made up its mind that I was a potential pilot, I expected the RAF to get on with any more training they wanted to give me. As usual, I was disappointed. I was sent to the Air Crew Holding Wing at Heaton Park in Manchester.

Heaton Park
When we arrived in Manchester, we found it populated by people who talked with a funny accent but we didn't expect to be there for long because as potential pilots, we knew that there was a shortage of trained personnel and it was obvious that we would be trained and thrown into the air war pretty quickly. Again – silly us! I was there at Heaton Park, on and off, for nearly two years. I say on and off because, initially they made sure that we had completed all the training which should have been completed at that stage, and then they sent us off to various RAF stations all over the country to make ourselves useful until there was a vacancy in the Empire Air Training Scheme. Under this setup, pilots were trained in Canada, Rhodesia, South Africa and the United States. It was complete pot luck where you were sent and it looked as though the aircrew cadets who wanted to go to a particular country were usually disappointed.

My first detachment from Heaton Park was to an airfield just outside York. It was a place called RAF Marston Moor and at that time it was the home of a Halifax bomber training unit. The Halifax was a four-engine bomber which, with the Lancaster, carried out most of the bombing raids on Germany. We were a training unit but when the Air Ministry decided to lay on a raid of 1,000 bombers, they had to call on the training units to make up the numbers. So from time to time all training stopped and the instructors and better students made up scratch crews to take part in raids on Germany. Most of my time here seemed to be spent on guard duty so I was not sorry when my detachment came to an end and I was returned to Heaton Park. As usual this was another false alarm and instead of going overseas, I was sent on yet another detachment.

This time I went to RAF Bardney in Lincolnshire. Here, there were lots of Lancasters and they were flown by one of the leading front-line squadrons. I was employed in the Armoury servicing gun turrets – I knew that my time at Nash & Thompson had not been wasted – and also preparing bomb loads before the squadron went off on raids over Germany. Since each of the 16 aircraft on the squadron carried 14 500-pound bombs, and each of these had to be taken out of storage, fitted with its 'tail', fitted with its detonator and pistol, and then taken out to the airfield and hand-winched up into the bomb bay, this represented a massive amount of manual labour. What made it worse was that either the Air Ministry, or someone at Bomber Command headquarters, frequently decided to change the bomb load. So down they all had to come – a harder job that fitting them – and another set of different size bombs then had to be prepared and fitted to the aircraft. On one memorable occasion, we changed the bomb load six times without any of the aircraft getting airborne. This was just after D Day when the targets changed quicker than we could mount the attacks. Our squadron, No 9 Squadron, was one of the first to get aircraft modified to carry the 22,000-pound 'grand slam' bomb. This was a huge, but very beautiful, bomb which was so large that it would not fit in the bomb bay and stuck out at the front and the rear. The aircraft were badly overloaded with all this weight on board but they still seemed to get airborne somehow.

Eventually, all good things come to an end and, in due course, I returned to Heaton Park, but this time it really was the real thing. After a few days we were shipped off to Liverpool Docks where we were marched on board the RMS *Andes*. This was a delightful, very new passenger liner which on this occasion had several thousand military passengers instead of its intended several hundred civilians. So it was a very tight fit. My draft were all in a space just above the propellers so it was a bit noisy to say the least. On departing Liverpool, we had an escort of two destroyers but, on the first night, the weather was so bad that the destroyers could not keep up with us and by the morning we were on our own. I was one of the very few guys who managed to surface for breakfast. The rest were suffering from the dreaded *mal de mer* and were lying in their hammocks feeling sorry for themselves. One of the things about seasickness is that if you give in to it, then it gets worse, but if you fight it then you can still operate and you gradually get better. 'Positive thinking' I believe is the name of the game. In later life I have found this again and again.

The *Andes* sped across the Atlantic and then ducked down into Freetown in Sierra Leone. Here we unloaded some of the troops and picked up some more fuel and some rations before setting off once more across the Atlantic and down to Cape Town. We disembarked there and got into a long troop train which was waiting to take us up to Bulawayo in Southern Rhodesia. This was the first time I had been out of Europe and it was a completely new world to most of us. The train journey took two long days and was pretty exhausting. Arriving at Bulawayo, we de-trained and went to a reception camp where we were allowed to acclimatise slowly.

They also refreshed our basic training and after a short
while, I was part of a group which was sent to an airfield at a
place called Mount Hampden. Here we were out in the bush
with no local amenities and so all we could do was get on
with the work. The aircraft used at these Elementary Flying
Training Schools was a machine called a Fairchild Cornell. It
looked rather like a modern-day Chipmunk. A low-wing
monoplane with a tail wheel. The cockpit had fore and aft
seating with the instructor in the back seat behind the
student. It was powered by an American Ranger engine
which gave it an adequate performance. We were able to get
on with our initial training here in relative comfort, with
none of the distractions which usually accompany a military
camp.

After a few months of this we had completed the course,
with only a few of our group dropping out and we were then
sent to Cranborne near Salisbury. This was a much larger
airfield and was within striking distance of the city, so the
distractions were back to spoil our training but to give us
somewhere to go in the evening and at the weekends. Training at the SFTS – Service Flying Training School – consisted
of some 250 hours flying on the North American Harvard
aircraft. This was an advanced trainer and turned out to be a
bit of a handful after the docile Cornell. Several pilots found
that they could not cope with the tendency of the aircraft to
swing on take off and landing and others found problems
with various other elements of the training. So several more
of our group were weeded out. Flying training consisted
initially of converting us to the very much more powerful
aircraft and then concentrated on such items as aerobatics,
dog fighting, low flying, navigation, formation flying and
night flying.

I have very clear recollection of a couple of incidents
which caused great hilarity among the young pilots under
training but which could have been total disasters if things
had not worked out as they did. The first occasion was when

we noticed that one of the students had taxied in, after a solo flight, sitting in the back seat. As I'm sure many of you realise, when a Harvard was flown solo, it was normally flown from the front seat, and the instructor sat in the back when we flew dual. One or two comments were made and that seemed to be that, until we noticed it happen again. And a third time. This was too much for us, so we asked the student about it.

'Oh it's quite easy,' he replied. 'You have to get up high enough to be clear of the turbulence and trim the aircraft very accurately at a nice low speed. Then you undo your harness and slide the parachute out of the seat. You will need to stand up and crouch in the well of the seat, facing aft. Next you lift the parachute and place it on the inter-decking between the seats. Now comes the tricky bit. You will need to open the front canopy and very carefully step out on to the port wing. Hold on tight and you will find that you can just reach the handle for the rear canopy, to unlock it and slide it aft. Now work your right leg over the cockpit side and using your right hand make a quick grab at the metal strut between the seats, then scramble into the rear cockpit and close the canopy. It will be a bit draughty with the front section of the hood open but it's not too bad. Now recover the parachute from the interdecking, place it on the seat, lower yourself into it and refasten the harness. Landing can be a bit tricky from the back but you soon get used to it.'

We were all very impressed. Particularly one character who looked thoughtful before disappearing into the hangar. A few days later he was scheduled to carry out a solo flight and off he went. Some 30 minutes later the aircraft reappeared. Its radio transmissions were dreadfully garbled, its flying was erratic in the extreme and the landing caused us all to wince. Looking at it, there seemed to be no one in it at all. Slowly the front canopy opened and a chalk-white face appeared. The pilot got out and sat on the ground. Even from 25 yards away we could all see that he was shaking like the proverbial aspen leaf. To cut a long story short, we helped him into the crew room and filled him with hot, strong and very sweet tea. It was many minutes before he said anything and slowly the story unfolded. He had indeed set the aircraft up, in trim, at low speed and high enough to be clear of the turbulence. He had removed his harness and parachute and he had stood up in the seat facing aft. He had hoisted his parachute on to the interdecking and he had opened the front canopy. He had stepped out on to the wing and when he reached for the rear canopy release, he had found it just out of his reach. And the slipstream was making it just about impossible for him to get forward again, to get back into the front cockpit. This is where lady luck smiled on him. Having moved himself as far aft as he could, he had made the aircraft slightly tail heavy and the aircraft had started to climb. This caused the speed to reduce and so enabled him to force himself forward against the blast of air, and get back into the front seat. Here he found that the parachute had fallen off the interdecking on to the floor of the rear cockpit where it was restricting the controls to a considerable degree. He was forced, therefore, to crouch on his seat and try and fly the aircraft back to base from that position. It's no wonder that his landing was more of an arrival than a landing. Everyone – bar one person – was very impressed by his story. The odd one out, as I expect you have guessed, was the cadet who had claimed to have done it three or four times before. After a decent interval he took the slowly recovering guy aside.

'Look, you idiot,' he said, 'that story was just to impress everyone. What I really do is land at one of the relief landing grounds, get into the back while I'm on the ground, take off again and fly back to base.'

If my memory serves me right, there was a complete sense of humour failure by the chap who had tried it in flight. Personally, I'd have killed the cadet who shot the initial line.

Another incident which sticks in my memory was the occasion when a solo cadet had an engine failure. He transmitted a distress call and proceeded to carry out a forced landing. Having picked a reasonable field, he set a himself up for the landing, but being young and very inexperienced, he misjudged it badly. Like all of us who have to do a forced landing 'in anger', rather than for practice, he overshot badly. The aircraft touched down a few yards in front of the hedge at the end of the field with an almighty bang, bounced back into the air, went over the hedge, and landed heavily on a very small field on the other side. With heavy braking, he managed to stop – just – without tipping it on its nose and got out badly shaken but unhurt. Meanwhile, one of the instructors who was airborne with his student had heard the distress call, flown to the field and spotted the student pilot with his aircraft in the very corner of a small triangular field. He pointed it out to his own student and remarked how well the unfortunate guy with the engine failure had done to get it into such a small field. Being of a helpful nature, the instructor decided to land in the field himself and see if there was some simple reason for the engine failure and forced landing. His student was somewhat worried.

'Rather a small field isn't it, sir?' he asked. 'Wouldn't it be easier to land in the bigger one next to it?'

'Don't worry,' was the reply, 'if a student can manage it, I'm sure I can!'

He proceeded to set his aircraft up for a landing. Crossing the hedge, just, he put the aircraft firmly down on the ground, braked heavily and managed to reduce his speed to some 20 miles per hour before he hit the previously undamaged aircraft in the corner of the field. As a result, two aircraft were severely damaged, but the only human injuries were the shock suffered by the original cadet whose aircraft had been safely, if heavily, landed after its engine failure, and the personal pride of the instructor who was flabbergasted to think that a student had managed a safe landing off a glide approach, while he couldn't manage a safe landing off a controlled approach with power available.

I went out to a Harvard one day intending to go and do some general handling. Start up was normal and the taxi out was normal. When I got round to the power checks, I was surprised to find that I had no mag drop at all (it should have been about 60–70 RPM on each Magneto). This had me a bit nonplussed because the main problem we came across was too large a mag drop, not too small a drop. The top limit was around 120 RPM and anything over that indicated a fouled plug. We did not go flying with a fouled plug. Being a cautious soul, I decided to ask someone better qualified than me, so I taxied back to the dispersal. I went and fetched the Flight Sergeant engineer and asked him to check the mags. He started up and ran the engine up. He called me over, and with the engine running, I climbed on the wing.

'What's the matter with that?' he asked. 'It's lovely and smooth.'

'Yes,' I replied, 'but what about this,' I said, turning both mags off. The engine continued to run perfectly well. His mouth opened.

'Yes, I see what you mean,' he said. Switching the engine off, he stuck his head under the instrument panel.

'Ah, I see where the problem is,' he said, 'the earth wire from the switch has come out.'

He re-connected it and tried again. This time there was a 'normal' mag drop. That day I learnt that no mag drop is almost worse than too big a mag drop. Later, I will tell you about another occasion many years later when the earth wire came out on another aircraft.

About two-thirds of the way through the course, I was

sent off on a cross-country flight. The weather was excellent and everything was going nicely. I had just turned on to the second leg and I knew where I was to within about a mile, so I could afford to relax. I did relax and that was a mistake because with the natural bloody-mindedness of inanimate objects, the engine picked on that moment to quit. This prompted the usual rush of adrenalin through the system and my hands flashed round the cockpit turning things on or off as the case might be. So I decided to try and restart the engine. I figured that the engine had cooled off after stopping and so I used the primer. At once the engine burst into life. And stopped again. So I primed again and once more it burst into life – and stopped again. After several such bursts, the penny dropped and the next time, I primed slowly and continuously. The engine restarted and kept going. Not very well, I must admit, but anything was better than nothing. I turned towards base and slowly made my way home. Priming with one hand and flying with the other. This meant that I didn't have a third hand to work the radio microphone, and I had to stop priming to get the wheels down. I set the aircraft up high and put the wheels down. Air Traffic having seen that I was on finals and had not been cleared to land, fired two or three Red Very lights to tell me to overshoot, but no way was I going around. I simply stopped priming, let the engine stop and carried out a glide landing on to the airfield. Air Traffic were scathing in their remarks about my having landed after getting a Red. I ignored them, because I was so glad to have got it on the ground without damaging myself or the aircraft. They saw that I was stationary on the airfield so the jeep was sent out to investigate and to tell me to get the aircraft off the runway. They didn't even apologise later when they got the facts from the jeep driver. Nobody but nobody apologises to a cadet pilot! When the engineers looked at it, they found that the mixture control had come disconnected and that the engine had slowly vibrated the mixture control to the cut-out position. For once, it was not my fault.

Another of the student pilots managed to achieve a bit of distinction following a navigation flight. During the course of training, we were required to fly a number of cross-country flights of various lengths and difficulty. In order that the staff should have some means of assessing our navigational skills we were always required to keep detailed logs of all our fixes, bearings, arrival times, heading changes and radio calls plus anything else which might be relevant. One guy was held up to ridicule one day when the navigation instructor produced his log card and asked what we thought of an idiot who put down a fix as being one mile north of a herd of elephants. Naturally we all laughed politely as we didn't want to fall out with the staff, but thinking about it later, was he really so stupid? The position of every herd of elephants was known to the game wardens and it would have been perfectly possible, knowing the time of the fix, to plot the most likely of the few alternative possible places and so find out where he had been. There were not many pinpoints in the Rhodesian bush. Maybe if he had described it as a 'running fix' the navigation instructor might have liked it better?

In 1944, one of my Instructors, Pilot Officer Pickett, taught me a trick which many years later was going to save my life. We had been discussing forced landings and he decided to demonstrate a technique for getting into a field after you have just undershot. It is a small technical cheat really but it works for me. He assumed that the aircraft making the forced landing was 'clean', that is to say did not have any flap down and was approaching the only field in the area. Let us also assume that the stalling speed with no flaps is 75 knots. The undershooting aircraft would approach at its best glide speed – whatever that might be – and then flare gently to try and reach the field. But the speed would reduce so that at 75 knots the wings would be unable to provide sufficient lift to keep the aircraft flying and it would fall to the ground, just short of the hedge. This can ruin your day. However, in the case of an aircraft with its flaps extended, it will have a considerably steeper angle of glide than a clean aircraft, but... The stalling speed with flaps down will be some 10–12 knots slower than the stalling speed with them up. So, at 76–77 knots, when he reaches a point just above the ground, the pilot flies level and selects flaps down. He can now fly on, still level, until his speed has reduced to the 'flaps down' stalling speed. This will often carry him into his field, and he is home and dry. He will come down much steeper after that, but if he has managed to get into the field he doesn't care.

I had a problem one day, some twelve years later, when I had a double engine failure in a Meteor aircraft at low level in the circuit at Kai Tak. The left engine failed just after I had initiated a missed approach and I was about half-way along the down-wind leg when the second engine flamed out. I turned hard towards the airfield and there is no doubt the aircraft would have managed to fly to within about 100 yards of the sea wall, which marked the edge of the airfield. The aircraft would have bounced once on the water, and then have rammed the sea wall. The stalling speed of a Meteor with no flap is 105 knots, but with flaps down, it is 85 knots. So at about 106 knots I suddenly remembered what I had been taught all those years ago in Rhodesia, and I selected 'flaps down'. The machine seemed to go on and on and on almost for ever – time seems to stand still in such cases – eventually, the wheels smacked down on the sea wall, some six to eight feet from the edge. The aircraft rolled across the grass, over the runway, across the grass on the other side of the runway, and so I turned left on to the taxi way. I didn't quite get as far as the dispersal so the ground crew had to push. I didn't help them, I reckoned that I had done enough. I had so much adrenalin in my bloodstream, it felt as though I had personally carried the aircraft for that last vital 100 yards.

Naturally, by the time we left Rhodesia, we were all getting very confident that we were the finest pilots in the world and it was probably a good thing that we should be very confident of our skills. It was only when we got on to our operational aircraft that we suddenly realised that we knew almost nothing about flying a fighting aircraft as opposed to a training aircraft.

Once we had got our wings, the Air Force shipped us back to the UK but not before we had spent a fortnight just outside Cape Town at a suburb called Muzenberg. It was only a 15-minute ride into the city on the train, and it had the most marvellous beaches packed with nubile young South African ladies. Heaven for relaxing RAF aircrew! All good things come to an end and after 14 days of bliss, we were marched on board the Cunard passenger liner *Aquitania*. The normal passenger complement was, I believe, about 800. In our case there were a few more. About 4.000 more. We filled the boat from bow to stern and the Mess Hall did not stop serving food at any time during the 24 hours. Most of the passengers were troops coming back from the Far East and so we were very small beer and were kept firmly in our place. The return trip took 14 days and we disembarked at Southampton. From here we were sent up to the holding unit at Market Harborough and then went on 14 days' leave.

At the end of my leave I reported to No 5 PAFU (Pilot Advanced Flying Unit) at RAF Hibaldstow. Once more we were flying the now familiar Harvard, and we were introduced to the problems of navigation and instrument flight in the UK. On completion of this refresher flying in the Harvard, we were converted on to the Spitfire. There is no doubt whatever that the Spitfire had a place in the heart of every pilot. It was reputed to be the most beautiful handling aircraft, it was delightful to look at and it even sounded special. The Rolls-Royce and the Packard, Merlin engines had a peculiar note to them that was unmistakable and even now, many, many years later, those of us who were lucky enough to fly them can still recognise the sound of a Spitfire from a long way away. That reputation was fully deserved. The conversion course consisted of lots of ground training to get to know all about the aircraft and some visits to the cockpit of an aircraft where we had to be able to find instantly each and every control lever or switch blindfolded. We each had a flight or two in the back seat of a Harvard to introduce us to the lack of visibility and prepare us for the curved approach path necessitated by the poor forward visibility on the ground in a Spitfire.

We had several Mark XVI Spitfires at Hibaldstow. These were a clipped-wing, low-level fighter variant with the Packard Merlin 266 engine, which was several times more powerful that the engines we were used to in the Harvard. One of the more common mistakes of new Spitfire pilots, was to take off with the throttle friction nut slightly slack. Once airborne, in order to raise the under-carriage, the pilot had to fly the aircraft with his left hand and select up with a rather complicated movement of the undercarriage selector lever on the right-hand side of the cockpit. This means that he had to release the throttle which he held in his left hand on take off. A split-second after changing hands, the throttle would slide shut and the engine would effectively stop. Instant panic, and the pilot would change hands back again and reopen the throttle. The aircraft would start to fly properly once more and he would try again, with the same result. This left two options. Either tighten the friction nut with the other hand, which meant letting go of the control column, or rushing the undercarriage up selection while the aircraft porpoises around the sky. It was very educational – people hardly ever did it more than once! One of the solutions, used exclusively by idiots, was to select 'up' when lined up on the runway and rely on the undercarriage squat switch to prevent the system from operating until the weight was off the wheels. Then, when the aircraft had flying speed, a firm lift off and the wheels came up automatically. This was fine if the switch was working – and it usually was – but even so, if you hit a bump during the take-off run and the switch freed the selector to raise the wheels, then... Yes, you've guessed it, the aircraft sank back on to the ground and the propeller struck the runway and bits went in all directions. We had four-bladed wooden propellers in those days and they flung hundreds of wood splinters for quite a distance. It looked very dramatic but it did nothing for the pilot's future in the RAF!

On 8 July 1946, it became my turn to fly in a Spitfire for the first time. I had a final session in the cockpit with the flight commander checking that I knew where everything was and, in due course. I started it up. Taxiing was not easy, there was this huge engine blocking the view, so we had to weave slowly from side to side to see where we were going. After completing my engine checks and pre-take-off checks, I lined up on the runway and slowly and carefully opened the throttle. I managed to remember that the propeller goes round in the opposite direction to the propeller in a Harvard, so the tendency was to swing to the right rather than to the left, I raised the tail slightly and before I knew what was happening, I was airborne. Waiting until I reached a safe height, I changed hands. Yes, I had remembered to tighten the friction nut on the throttle – and I selected the undercarriage 'up'. Climbing straight ahead I went up to about 10,000 feet and tried a few turns and things like that and then set off to return to base. I found the airfield, called on the radio to tell them that I was rejoining and entered the circuit pattern. Looking at my engine temperature gauge, I found it just below the red line and this had me a bit worried. I knew that the undercarriage leg when lowered, blanks the radiator off and I feared that when I lowered it, the engine might boil before I could land and taxi back. Having mulled over this problem, I decided to climb back up to 3,000 feet and then close the throttle and glide into the circuit and so cool the engine down. This worked very well and I was able to lower the undercarriage, land and taxi back. As soon as I had parked, I switched the engine off and was relieved to find that it didn't boil. The flight commander came rushing over. 'Did you have to use the emergency system?' he asked.

'No,' I replied.

'Jolly good,' he said, 'I told the guys in the tower to keep quiet. I said that you would be able to sort it out and not to distract you with gratuitous help which you didn't need. Come and have a coffee.'

We walked back to the crew room together. I had always been aware that there was a special relationship among Spitfire pilots, but this was the very first time I had ever seen or heard a flight lieutenant talk to a sergeant pilot as though he was a human being, let alone an equal. Naturally, being modest (!) I didn't boast about my flight. It's probably just as well because about a week later I found out that on the first occasion that I joined the circuit, my starboard undercarriage leg had been down and the port one up. That was why the engine was overheating. The Control Tower thought that I had selected the under-carriage down and only one leg had come down. So when I climbed up again for my glide to cool the engine, they thought that I had known what I was doing. I never did let on that I hadn't noticed that the starboard leg had been down for the whole flight. My second solo, four days later was uneventful, but of course, I was twice as experienced by then.

Hibaldstow, in Lincolnshire, is famous throughout the Royal Air Force as the airfield where 'they give rides to

WAAFs on the tail of the aircraft'. Naturally the story was better than the real facts. When we were doing our full power checks, the engine was so powerful that it was necessary to have someone lying across the tail to keep it on the ground. Normally these people would get off after the power check and, assuming that everything was OK with the engine, the pilot would then take off. On one particular occasion, a young WAAF was lying on the tail and for some reason or other she didn't get off when the pilot had completed his checks. The aircraft taxied onto the runway and proceeded to take off. I gather that this extra passenger flight was noticed by Air Traffic who instructed the pilot to complete a circuit and land. The poor lass on the tail was being held by the slipstream and I have no doubt that she was gripping anything she could hold on to with a grip of iron. After landing the pilot was told to stop. An ambulance drove up and removed the girl from the tail. They did not tell the pilot about his passenger while he was in the air as they didn't want him to panic and worry about the strange handling with this extra weight on the tail. I gather that lady concerned has been able to dine out on the story ever since. And she jolly well deserves to!

A month later I arrived at No. 61 OTU at Keevil in Wiltshire where I completed my operational training on Spitfires before being posted to a front-line squadron. It was at Keevil that we learned how to fight the aircraft, how to shoot, and how to fly in formation, and the more we flew it, the more we realised what a superbly designed aircraft it was. I didn't get the opportunity to fly Spitfires for very long, indeed for not nearly long enough, but there is no doubt that it was one of the high spots in my flying career.

While I was at Keevil I bought my first motor vehicle, a 350 cc Ariel motorcycle. I and two or three other guys used to ride around the local area whenever we could get any petrol. I'm glad I had that machine, because without it I would not have gone swimming in Trowbridge on the last day the pool was open in 1946. It was really far too cold for swimming but being young and foolish – not to mention overconfident – we persisted. I didn't stay in the water for very long and neither did my three friends. We were soon clustered round the tea bar, warming ourselves up on a nice hot cup of sweet tea. I happened to wander to the edge of the pool where there were one or two other swimmers. One of these was a young girl about seven or eight years old. I noticed that her sister was standing near the edge and then I realised that tears were rolling down her face. Being the perennial Nosy Parker, I asked her what the matter was. She pointed to her big sister and said: 'I told her not to go in the deep bit … she can't swim.' I looked, the sister was floating face down in the water looking at the bottom, and not moving. Being quick on the uptake it finally dawned on me that all was not well so I dropped my cup and saucer and jumped into the pool beside the floating girl. My jump took me straight to the bottom so, pushing off with my feet, I came up fast beside the floating girl and in effect propelled her out of the water on to the nearby side of the pool. My friends had heard the crash of my cup breaking so they came to the edge and helped lift her the rest of the way out of the pool. Several pints of water came out of her mouth and she coughed and spluttered a bit before bursting into tears. The pool attendant came bustling over and wanted to know who had broken the cup. 'You will have to pay for it you know!' was the sum total of his contribution. My reply was very short, just two words, which I leave to your imagination. The lady from the ladies' changing room then came hurrying over then and took the two children away and I and my friends decided to leave.

Once we had completed the operational training course at Keevil we were all posted to our first Operational Fighter Squadron. In my case, this turned out to be No. 20 Squadron in India.

2

Tempests: 1947–49

After a bit of research, I found out where No. 20 Squadron was based. It was located at Agra, about 100 miles south-south-east of Delhi. To get there involved a cruise on a troop ship through the Mediterranean, down the Suez Canal, along the Red Sea and across to Karachi. Here we were shepherded into a magnificent example of the Indian State Railways and we proceeded steadily on our way to Delhi. After spending the best part of a day in Delhi, I was put on another train and a few hours later arrived at Agra, to be met by a small vehicle which took me the three or four miles out to the airfield. I hadn't really thought about it, but having been trained on Spitfires, I expected the squadron to be equipped with Spitfire aircraft, but that only goes to show how simple I am. When I introduced myself to the squadron commander I was surprised to notice that they had a long line of Mark II Tempests, but no Spitfires. In order to convert new pilots such as myself, there was a squadron Harvard and we were given a couple of trips in the back seat to familiarise us with the local area and to simulate the handling of the Tempest. The local area was quite different to anything I had ever seen before. To the east of the airfield

25

was the town of Agra with the Red Fort on the bank of the river Jumna and a bit up river from the town was the Taj Mahal. Truly one of the Seven Wonders of the World, it is the most wonderful structure I have ever seen. From an aircraft, in particular, one can see it in its entirety. I can only imagine what it would have been like if the second tomb, in black marble, had been built on the opposite bank of the river. It was a very short-sighted decision which was made, when the Emperor Shah Jehan died, to put his body alongside that of his wife in the Taj Mahal and not in the black marble duplicate on the other side of the river.

I have nothing but happy memories of my time flying Tempests. The Mark II was fitted with an air-cooled engine and so was far more suitable in hot climates than the liquid-cooled versions, since it did not have the ability to boil. The Centaurus engine was the most complicated device I have

Tempest Mk II, a very low-level fighter!

Tempest Mk II at Agra

ever come across. It was a multi-cylinder radial engine with sleeve valves – with all the moving, sliding, twisting bits which that involved, but with a two speed two stage supercharger, with intercooler, it turned out an awful lot of power and, speaking from my personal experience, it was fully reliable. With a propeller of over 14 feet diameter, it was a bit of a handful on take off – indeed we needed to use port brake in the early stages of the take off run in order to keep straight – but once in the air, it flew like a real gentleman. As a weapons platform, all marks of Tempests were absolutely rock steady and it was possible to aim its principal weapon, the three inch drainpipe rocket with a 60 lb warhead, with astonishing accuracy. The aircraft was immensely strong and was just about unbreakable. While I was there, I managed to learn enough Hindi to make myself understood but with the passing of time many of my

27

memories of India seem to have faded although one or two occurrences still stick in my memory. I will tell you about some of the incidents which I remember from my time there.

At Agra, many of our meals were eaten out of doors. One of the disadvantages of this was that the local population of kites, a large local hawk, knew exactly when and where we were likely to eat and they assembled in their formations waiting to pillage our meals. Their technique was to swoop down as we walked to our tables and snatch the meat off the plates. Putting a cover over the meal didn't work for long as they just used to knock the plate out of our hands, on to the ground and then snatch the nice juicy meat. We decided one day that something must be done. The next day saw a steady stream of pilots carrying plates, walking to the shaded area where the tables were all set out. This time we didn't try to stop the theft of food from our plates. What the kites didn't know was that we had prepared some special 'fighter pilot meals' for them. Naturally, the assembled birds soon started the attack. With their normal high-speed dive, they arrived and grabbed the small piece of meat on the plate. It was then they found out what we had done. No, nothing which might hurt them. After all, they flew almost as well as we did. What we did do, was attach a small model aircraft to the meat by means of a 3–4 foot length of strong twine. After their attack, off went the kites clutching our bits of meat, hotly pursued by a small 'RAF fighter'. When the bird swung its feet forward to reach the meat with its beak in order to eat it, it saw the pursuing 'fighter aircraft'. Instant panic! But no matter how hard they weaved, climbed, turned or man-oeuvred, they couldn't shake off their pursuing RAF fighter. Within 15 minutes, the sky was full of dog-fighting kites, each with its own personal RAF fighter on its tail. It was some time before we all stopped laughing and the sky slowly cleared. I have no idea how long the birds hung on to the meat but every time they looked, nemesis in the form of an RAF fighter, complete with roundels, was following them. Strangely, there was a shortage of kites in the vicinity of the camp after that.

Animals seem to figure largely in my memories of India. It was very much a local custom to rest in the heat of the day and after lunch (*tiffin* to you) I frequently stretched out on my bed (*charpoy* to the locals) and rested my eyelids. There were a number of flying insects in the area and there was fly netting over the windows which was supposed to keep them out. This was not very efficient so we used to encourage the small house lizards to adopt our rooms. I had a couple, who used to patrol my room and they kept the place pretty clear of anything which flew. One day, having eaten well, I stripped off and was resting my eyelids, while I lay on my back on the *charpoy* and was soon fast asleep. The larger of my lizards was on the wall to the right of my head. The *charpoy* was positioned in the corner of the room against the wall which was on my left-hand side and unbeknown to me a large juicy insect landed about half-way up the wall, approximately level with my ankles. My guardian lizard had spotted this landing and decided that it would make a nice lunch. With no more ado, the lizard launched himself in the direction of his meal. This was a diagonal track starting on my right shoulder, across my chest in a straight line across my naked sweaty body, to my left knee from where he launched himself up the wall. The shock to my system triggered a hurried reaction and I think I passed the lizard about half-way up the wall. I swear I must have reached the ceiling first, not from a 'standing' start but a 'lying on my back' start! If there had been records for 'vertical accelera-tion' I would have easily broken the world record. Or would the lizard have counted as outside assistance?

Another typical RAF 'sport' took place in the evening. The local road into town passed close to the camp and after a few beers it was considered to be a good local game to wander to the roundabout by the camp entrance. Here convoys of ox-carts plodded slowly towards town, aiming for the morning market. The animals were trained to follow the one in front, so we would wait until a suitable sized convoy arrived and then without waking the driver of the lead vehicle who was sleeping happily, we would lead his ox round until it reached the back of the last wagon. This it would then follow. In the morning, when one of the drivers woke up he would be a bit surprised to see that all the oxen had been following the cart ahead all night in a circle round the same roundabout.

There was another RAF squadron of Tempests in India who were based at Rawalpindi and, periodically, we used to send a couple of aircraft up there on a visit. The 'official' reason for the flights was to provide navigational practice and for an exchange of operational techniques and ideas. However there was another reason. At Rawalpindi, there was a very good local brewery and it seemed very unprofessional to ignore the fact. So steps were taken to take advantage of the location of this brewery. The aircraft going up there used to carry long-range drop tanks. Three of these were used to carry petrol but the fourth was a highly polished (internally) and sterilised container which was used to transport 90 gallons of best beer all the way back to Agra. As you can imagine, this had a very beneficial effect on the morale of my squadron.

Eventually, the politicians decided that the partition of British India was a 'good thing' and so the nations of India and Pakistan were formed. So far as we were concerned, we were surplus to requirements and so the squadron was disbanded. The aircraft were presented to the Indian and Pakistan governments (one squadron to each), and we pilots were all shipped home. But not before we had spent some time 'resting', first at Karachi and later at Bombay, from where we boarded another troopship and returned to the UK. Here I was sent on 14 days' leave at the end of which I had to report at Southampton for shipment. I was destined to board yet another troop ship which was to take me to

Port Said in order to join No. 213 Squadron, which formed part of No. 324 Mobile Wing.

Moving on now to the Middle East, I spent my first few days at the reception camp at El Hamra. This was to give us a chance to acclimatise to the heat before moving to Khartoum in the Sudan. It was a most uncomfortable tented camp where everything was covered with sand or flies or both and I was glad to get out of it and on my way south. Khartoum lies on the east bank of the Nile, with the village of Omdurman opposite it on the west bank. It was famous for the defence of the city by General Kitchener and its later relief by General Gordon. There are statues of both of these generals in the town. I had found it extremely hot in central India but it was a great deal hotter in the Sudan and in those days there was no air conditioning but we survived somehow. The aircraft were not quite the same as the ones I had been flying in India. They were the Mark VI version which has the liquid-cooled Napier Sabre engine. This was a 24-cylinder engine with two crankshafts and the cylinders in four rows of six forming in effect two flat 12-cylinder engines. Tucked on the back was the two-speed, two-stage supercharger (with intercooler) and on the front the very large radiator. Being a tropicalised version of the Mark V aircraft, there was an additional oil cooler mounted in the leading edge of the port wing. This engine gave a massive amount of power but was pretty reliable.

My first flight was intended to be a familiarisation flight to get used to the new type of aircraft and to have a look round the local flying area. In the event it was not to work out like that. When I took off, I made sure that I held the aircraft down, to pick up climbing speed, and when I raised the nose I looked at the air speed indicator. It was either reading 'zero' or '360 knots'. Both were very unlikely so it seemed probable that I had no airspeed indicator. Naturally, the first thing I did was to check to see if I had left the cover on the pitot head. I hadn't! That helped my reputation but did nothing to help me land the beast. I called on the radio and asked the Tower to contact the squadron and ask them to get someone airborne for me to formate on so that I could have some indication of my speed when I came in to land. About 20 minutes later, I saw an aircraft taxi out and when airborne he called me. It was Flight Lieutenant Les Lunn, my flight commander. He suggested that I closed on him and practised my formation flying and then in a while he would make an approach to land and overshoot at the last moment, leaving me to land. So that was what we did. When the time to land arrived, I made sure that I was slowly overtaking the other aircraft and when he overshot, I closed my throttle slowly and hoped for the best. I ended up with a complete anti-climax and it all became a non-event. (I like them.) When we looked, the plumbing inside the port wing had come disconnected, hence the 'no airspeed'. That is the sort of hassle I could well have done without on my first solo on type.

Being part of a Mobile Wing, there were a number of incidents and detachments which have stuck in my memory and taking them in approximately chronological order, my first memory is of one fine sunny day when I was airborne from Khartoum in the Sudan to do some general handling. Also at Khartoum on detachment was the prototype of the single-seat Vampire jet fighter which had gone there to complete its tropical trials. On this particular day, the Vampire had gone off to do some fuel consumption tests. All was reasonably serene until about three-quarters of an hour into my flight. Suddenly I heard a call on the radio. It was from the Vampire pilot. He had been so engrossed in his trial and in ensuring that his flying and his fuel figures were accurate, that he had omitted to turn round and he was now so far away that he didn't have enough fuel to get home. I must add here that all the early jet fighters, which includes the Vampire and even more so the Meteor, had very short-range fuel tanks and we regularly ran them down to less than five minutes' reserve. Anyhow, to return to the Sudan,

Khartoum Tower gave him a heading to steer to get home and told him that there were no airfields south of Khartoum. This was in 1948, remember. The Vampire pilot used his remaining fuel to get as far as he possibly could and then when the engine finally ran out, he glided, still on course, for Khartoum. The Vampire is an excellent glider, we used to get better than three miles per thousand feet in a glide and, as he was around 30,000 feet when the engine stopped, he managed an extra 100 miles just gliding. Meanwhile, I and another pilot who had also heard the radio calls, positioned ourselves along his track until we spotted him and then we trailed on behind his aircraft like a pair of vultures. It was evident that he was not going to be able to reach Khartoum and he announced that he intended to bail out. This seemed to be a bit of a waste of an aircraft. So we informed him smartly that the Wing's weapons' range was only about a mile from him and the ground there was flat and hard, hard enough to take a three-ton lorry with no difficulty and definitely hard enough to take his aircraft. He turned towards the bombing range and after lowering the undercarriage and flaps by use of the emergency system, he carried out a very nice landing with no damage at all to the aircraft. Meanwhile back at base, a fuel tanker was got ready and together with a light truck to carry a starter trolley, the rescue convoy set off. After about an hour's drive they reached the Vampire and filled the tanks about half full. This was more than enough to get him safely home, so the starter trolley was plugged in, the engine was started, and in a cloud of sand, he took off again and returned to Khartoum, a somewhat embarrassed test pilot.

Being a Mobile Wing, we were always ready to move at very little notice and, on 3 April 1948, the squadron was ordered to send a detachment to Asmara, the main town in Eritrea. The aircraft and ground crew were rapidly on their way, together with many cases full of spares and ammunition. We had to commandeer a BOAC Dakota to help carry the ground crew. I didn't go on the first wave but followed on 15 April. Each aircraft returned to Khartoum when it was due for routine servicing and a practice had grown up of buzzing the airfield at Asmara before returning to base. A few days after arriving, I was detailed to take an aircraft back, so, being in those days both young and foolish, I decided that I would give them the beat up to end all beat ups. Nowadays, I'm not nearly so young but probably just about as foolish! Anyhow, I went to the far corner of the airfield, applied full power, released the brakes, raised the tail, and in due course got airborne. Holding the aircraft parallel to the surface of the airfield, I raised the undercarriage and was then able to descend (slightly). Maintaining full power, and lining up with the crew room, I let the aircraft accelerate. The Tempest is probably the fasting accelerating aircraft ever built, and the 0–300 time is amazingly short – certainly much better than modern jets – and I was going very fast when I reached the buildings. Leaving it to the last moment, I pulled up, over the crew room and went on my way, with a couple of climbing rolls for good measure. Apparently my wake vortex caused the whole of the wooden hut to jump some two inches into the air. This was not a popular move. I continued my way blissfully unaware of the displeasure behind me. After a while, the radiator temperature got a bit higher than usual and I eased the throttle back slightly to help cool it down a little. This caused me to slow down and, as a result, the air flow through the radiator was reduced and the temperature rose again. So I had to descend slowly to keep the speed up. Unfortunately, this meant that I was getting into hotter air, and it really is hot in the Sudan. So the temperature went up again, and up and up. Finally, Khartoum appeared on the horizon and I called for a straight-in approach. This was approved and I landed, leaving the undercarriage and flaps to the very last moment. As the aircraft settled itself on to the runway and the airflow ceased, so the temperature rapidly increased until at 130 degrees Centigrade all the safety disks blew out and the front of the aircraft was enveloped in a ball of steam and glycol. Undoing my straps, I nipped round to the front, and, to my horror, I found the radiator was full of grass which I had picked up in my run across the airfield at Asmara. Quickly I grabbed most of it and dumped it away from the aircraft, hidden from the Tower by the ball of steam. Back at Asmara, the other pilots looked at the airfield and noticed a groove where my propeller had cut a swathe in the long grass, pointing directly at the crew room hut. For some reason or other, beat ups were banned after that. I can't think why.

Shifta hunting

Shortly after our arrival in Eritrea we were asked to lay on a fire-power demonstration for the local chiefs and head men. There was an escarpment some 20 miles away which made a natural grandstand and about half of a mile from it was a small densely wooded hill. The dummy scenario was that a bunch of *shifta* (bandits) had been reported to be hiding on the wooded hill, and the aircraft would be called in to flush them out to where loyal troops were waiting. The head men were all gathered on the edge of the escarpment and our Army Liaison officer (Captain Claud Histed of the South Staffordshire Regiment) called us in over the radio. The squadron had six aircraft on detachment in Eritrea and we attacked singly, in line astern. The first attack was a salvo of eight rockets from each aircraft and the second attack was a strafing run firing four 20-millimetre cannon from each aircraft. It was quite an impressive attack with lots of noise and smoke, but what made it infinitely more impressive and very much convinced all the chiefs and head men of our importance and skill was the fact that a band of about 40 *shifta* scuttled out of the back of the woods and took to their heels. Unbeknown to anyone, there really was a band of them hiding on that hill.

One morning at Asmara, another pilot and I were on the

early shift so we were in the crew room when the red phone rang. Scramble! We nipped out to the aircraft which we had prepared earlier, climbed in and set off. As soon as we were airborne, Air Traffic told us where to go and we were informed that a gang of *shifta* had raided several villages during the night and stolen all their cattle. The herd was heading towards Ethiopia and the pursuing forces didn't expect to catch up with them before they got across the border. Could we help? We pressed on to the area while I thought about this. When we got there we had no problem finding the stolen cattle. The herd was a large one and it was being driven hard so there was a good dust cloud. I had a bright idea. Turning my guns on, I put a line of 20-millimetre high explosive shells across the front of the cattle just a few yards ahead of them. They didn't seem to like this, so they stopped, turned round and ran in the opposite direction as if their lives depended on it. Every time a bunch of them looked like slowing down, a short burst of cannon fire soon got them going again. We managed to scatter the herd to 'hell and high water' as the saying goes. As a result, almost all the cattle were recovered later by their lawful owners. Cattle are the main currency of the area, so these flocks represented most of the wealth of the villages concerned.

During the squadron's detachment from Khartoum to Asmara, we gave air support to a locally raised force of troops. These were the genuine 'fuzzy wuzzies' of the days of Kitchener and General Gordon. They had heavily greased bouffant hair styles, hence the name. They also happened to be very fierce tribal soldiers. When the local troubles were considered over, there was a farewell parade for these locally enlisted troops. They received their pay for the campaign but first they had to hand in their rifles and the 50 rounds of ammunition with which they had been issued. When they had been in action, they had to retain the empty cartridge cases in order to be issued with replacements. After the parade, there was a march past followed by a 'charge past' in which the entire native force sprinted past the reviewing party, brandishing their rifles and screaming the most bloodthirsty expressions. Then the rifles were handed in, the ammunition counted and the pay issued. Then the real party started. The various members of the force vied with each other to produce the wildest tribal dances. And these were for the benefit of the dancers not for the benefit of tourists, so they were the real thing. I was one of the four or five RAF pilots invited to attend the parade, so I got a first hand view of it all. During a bit of a lull in the proceedings I wandered about the camp and I happened to notice a group of 12 guys who didn't seem to be enjoying the festivities. Still being the perennial Nosy Parker, I found our interpreter and asked him: 'Who are those people and why are they not taking part in the fun and games?'

'What people, sir?' he asked, looking puzzled.

'Those 12 over there in the white clothing,' I replied.

'I'm sorry, sir,' he answered, 'but there is nobody over there.' And he walked off.

This had me a bit nonplussed so I took a photograph of them and went to discuss them with one of the other pilots. Something delayed me and it was a while before I got back to where the 12 men had been standing. Sure enough there was no one there. It was only later that I heard that the local forces didn't take prisoners. These 12 had been a group of *shifta* who had been caught. About five minutes after my initial sighting, I gather they were taken round the back of the camp and beheaded. It's no wonder they didn't look as though they were enjoying the party. As far as the inter-preter was concerned, they were dead men and so didn't exist. Which is why he couldn't see them. They were non-persons. I think I am probably the only person ever to take a photograph of *shifta* prisoners.

We had some interesting trips while we were at Asmara. On one such trip we were taken to visit a village in the hills which was also the site of a monastery. The village was

The road to the Monastery, Eritrea

much the same as any other village but the monastery was an extraordinary feat of engineering. The 'road' to the monastery consisted of a footpath some 18 inches wide along the top of a ridge between two mountains. The monastery was on the far mountain and there was no other way up to it. The cliffs were reported to be unclimbable. Everything needed to build, furnish, equip or supply the monastery had to be carried along this 'road'. The rock sloped down at 45 degrees on both sides for over 200 yards and, yes, in answer to our question, people frequently fall off, or get blown off by the wind. This was believed to show that the people concerned had led less than perfect lives so was only to be expected. We did not volunteer to cross over. Somehow I feel that some of the monks stayed in the monastery because they couldn't face the return trip.

The next incident occurred on my birthday (14 July 1948). My aircraft had been off line with some technical snag so I borrowed the squadron commander's aircraft. The oxygen needed to be re-filled but apart from that the aircraft was on top line. We took off as a section of four aircraft and I was in the number three position. For those who are not familiar with the finger-four formation. The leader's number two man flies on one side of him and the number three on his other side. My own number two (Red 4) formated outside me. When in a battle formation we stayed in the same layout but much further out and during turns of more than 45 degrees, we crossed over/under the leader and so ended up on the other side. During the climb up to our operating altitude, which was to have been about 25,000 feet, I was on the leader's right with my own number two outside me. The aircraft were spaced with the wing tips not quite overlapping and I was about six to ten feet behind the leader. As we passed about 16,000 feet, my number two reported that I seemed to fall over in the cockpit, and my aircraft slowly rolled to the right and went on rolling. He took evasive action and followed me down. As he passed an altitude of 3000 feet, he says he was doing well over 500 knots (575 mph) and my aircraft was pulling away and still rolling. He pulled out fairly hard to avoid hitting the ground. It was at about this time that I woke up, looked up, saw trees growing downwards, didn't believe it, rolled the right way up and pulled very hard on the control column. My hands must have remembered to pull for long enough, because my next recollection is finding myself at some 6000 feet with the aircraft hanging on its prop and wallowing near the stall. The rest of the formation, which had been following us rather more circumspectly, noticed a plume of dust which they thought was my aircraft striking the ground. It wasn't. It was the wake vortex stirred up by my manoeuvre. There is no doubt that I must have been a long way below 200 feet at the bottom and was probably well under 50 feet. I went out like a light from the 'G' and I don't know what loading the aircraft reached because the accelerometer broke when it reached double figures, but it was well over the permitted +6G and was probably around the 12–14G figure. When I regained consciousness, at about 6000 feet with the aircraft hanging on its propeller and wallowing like a pig, I hadn't a clue what was going on so I called the other aircraft. The formation leader instructed me to return to base and land. Slowly I gathered my wits about me, remembered Khartoum, found the airfield and called the Tower to let them know that I had a major problem and wanted a priority landing. They informed me that a Brigand aircraft (2-engine light bomber/ground attack aircraft) was back-tracking the runway and I could not land. This stimulated a rather blunt message from me, telling them to get him out of the way because I was going to land anyhow. I did. The Brigand turned off the runway on to soft sand and took a long time to be dug out. Shortly after crossing the edge of the airfield, I saw the Air Traffic building, a two-storey red and white chequered affair, fly across the runway. It was followed by a second one. I didn't believe it and leant on the engine cut out. I regained consciousness in the ambulance. The aircraft had just rolled to a standstill without further damage. A careful investigation determined that the oxygen which had been put into my aircraft – or rather the squadron commander's aircraft – had been contaminated. There was still a load of CTC (Carbon-tetrachloride) in it. A mix of CTC and oxygen produces a lethal gas called Phosgene. That is what I had been breathing. The aircraft's oxygen system is designed to give you very little extra oxygen at low level but more and more as you get higher. At 16,000 feet, there was enough to make me lose consciousness. I was not a pretty sight when they recovered me from the aircraft, but I got 14 days' sick leave out of it, and the squadron commander's aircraft was written off. The wings looked like corrugated iron, they had so many wrinkles. But somehow they had stayed attached to the aircraft.

While I am talking about my time at Khartoum, it is perhaps worth mentioning that one of the training aids used by a the Royal Air Force to teach fighter pilots the skills of shooting at moving targets was the clay pigeon range. At Khartoum there was no clay pigeon installation but instead, the pilots were shipped up river to a government rest house at a place called Jebel Aulia. There was a dam here across the Nile to form a vast lake and there were some of the largest perch in the world resident in the spillways. It was not uncommon for them to run to over 150 pounds and they made a useful addition to the food in the Messes. The official reason for sending the crews of the resident fighter squadron down here for the weekend was to enable them to practise their shooting skills on the vast flocks of duck and geese that lived in the area. The unofficial reason for sending us there was so that we could have a really relaxing time and let our hair down without anyone around to complain. We drove to the rest house and unloaded all our kit by about 3 pm and then the shotguns were issued together with a large stock of ammunition. We proceeded in a non-military manner to the area where we would get the best of the evening flights of duck and geese. Each pilot was accompanied by one or two of the local Sudanese boys, aged about 8–12 years old, who acted as spotters of incoming flights and also as retrievers of any birds unlucky enough to be shot down. These lads had quite remarkable eyesight. They could spot a duck or a 'whizzer' (goose) at the most phenomenal ranges and they encouraged us to open fire while the birds were at about 200 yards' range. Needless to say we took the bait and blazed away with both barrels, and on many occasions had time to reload twice before the birds had passed us. Very occasionally we managed to hit one and inevitably one's rank went up when this happened. By dark most of us were at least 'colonels' and one guy was even a 'general'. This was the moment when we returned to the rest house and sampled the rations. Oddly enough there were several cases of hard liquor, not to mention many boxes of beer. (The water was considered unfit to drink and shooting is thirsty work.) After a large meal, we retired to bed, only to be woken up at 3 am to get out to catch the morning flights. Needless to say, the shooting was even less accurate than it had been during the previous evening and at about nine o'clock we returned to the rest house for breakfast. While we waited for the evening flights some of us used to put a line into the dam sluices with a spinner on the end of it, and try to catch one of the huge Nile perch. Sometimes we succeeded but more often than not we failed. This process continued all weekend, Friday, Saturday and Sunday, but after the evening flight on Sunday, we all climbed back into the trucks and returned to Khartoum. I don't know if it improved our shooting but it was a hell of a good way to spend a weekend. But our turn only came round about once every three months.

The other animals with which we came into contact were

both inhabitants of the Nile. For those who don't know about the Nile, south of Khartoum, it consists of two rivers. The Blue Nile which comes down from the hills of Ethiopia and the White Nile which comes up through the Southern Sudan, having risen in Uganda. The reason for these names, strangely enough, is because the Blue Nile is lovely, clear, clean water and looks blue in colour, and the White Nile has particles of clay in suspension and is definitely 'white' in colour. The two rivers meet at Khartoum and flow north eventually reaching the sea at the Nile delta north of Cairo. The waters of the Blue and White Niles do not mix for a long time and for several miles the right-hand bank of the river has 'blue' water and is safe for bathing and the left side is milky 'white' and is unsafe. Safe in this context means safe from the bilharzia snail. This little chap lives in the waters of the White Nile and carries a parasite which can get into the body. There it affects the liver – and other parts – and does the person no good at all. The solution is simple: bathe in the Blue Nile if you wish but never in the White Nile. However, that is not all the story. There are also beasts known as crocodiles. They are ugly, hungry, patient and lethal if they decide to take a bite. They tend to grow to very large size in the Nile – 15 feet is not unknown and they certainly like red meat. They live quite a long time and I understand that they have not evolved significantly for several thousand years and are much the same as they were in prehistoric times. One of the training exercises which we developed, was for our Army Liaison Officer to take a trip down the Nile and find a village where the headman had reported that the crocodiles were a nuisance and kept killing villagers. We would then organise a shoot. But a shoot with a difference. Instead of rifles, we used 20-millimetre cannon. We would treat the crocodiles as 'enemy tanks or soft skinned vehicles' and the Army Liaison Officer would call down an air strike which then proceeded to strafe the animals. Many were killed in this manner and the locals all approved and sent profuse thanks for reducing the dangers of living on the banks of the Nile. Not only was it good fun and helpful to the local residents but it was very good training for our operational role.

On 17 August 1948, the squadron was sent to Mogadishu to cover the withdrawal of British forces from the Ogaden, an area between Somalia and Ethiopia. On arrival, the airfield was very much as it had been when the Italian Air Force left it in a hurry, several years earlier. We soon set about getting it habitable for humans and the CO gave me a job which I could well have done without. Behind the flight buildings and offices, there was a very large privy – what is described as 'a 24 holer'. It stank to high heaven and was several feet deep in what I can best describe as slurry. On top of the 'slurry' was a layer about three feet thick of flies and maggots. I was tasked to remove or otherwise make it sanitary. This posed quite a problem. The pit was lined with rocks and had stood, festering slowly, for several years. I thought about this and finally came to a decision. Returning to the flight line, I scrounged about 30 gallons of waste oil and about 10 gallons of 130 octane petrol. This was all poured carefully down one of the 24 openings in the wooden, and partially rotten, top of the pit and we all returned to a safe distance, having left several of the lids in an open position. Armed with a 'two star red' distress flare, I took careful aim and fired. The first flare was all that was needed. There was an almighty Whoosh! and 24 columns of flame shot into the air accompanied by most of the remaining 24 lids. It was a highly dramatic ending to a most insalubrious installation. Not only that, but the fire burned for over an hour by which time it had destroyed the vast number of maggots and flies in the pit completely and, at the end of this time, the rock walls finally gave up the ghost and fell in to the pit neatly sealing it. Very little was needed in the way of tidying up and the CO was quite pleased with me for once.

Eventually the detachment came to an end. The Ogaden

was handed over with no problems and the squadron was directed to move up to Deversoir in the Canal Zone where it was due to join the rest of the Wing. When we were all ready, the squadron set off on the first leg which took us to Aden. Here we were scheduled to night stop, continuing north, to the Canal Zone, the next day with a refuelling stop at Port Sudan, about half-way up the Red Sea. The following morning several of the aircraft, including mine, went unserviceable for some reason or other and rather than wait until they were fixed, the squadron commander told me to wait at Aden until they were all serviceable and then bring them up to Deversoir. It was nearly midday before we were all ready and off we went, arriving at Port Sudan at about three o'clock in the afternoon. Here we eventually managed to get refuelled but by then it was too late to get to Deversoir before dark, and in those days, night flights were prohibited over the Canal Zone. As a result we all moved into the Port Sudan Hotel, together with the pilots of three more aircraft which had developed technical problems at Port Sudan. I now had eight aircraft in my care. Early the next morning a Dakota landed just before a tremendous storm broke. This had the effect of making the mud runway into a sludge runway and there was no possibility of anyone being able to get airborne until the runway dried. Local opinion was that it would take three to four days to dry out. Fortunately, the Dakota which landed had been carrying some of our own ground crew up to Deversoir so we were able to get the sick aircraft serviced while we waited. On the third day, I decided to have a look at the runway. The pilots drove up to the airfield and we all walked along the runway in line abreast. The up-wind end of the runway was still soft but I decided that there was just enough of it that had dried out to enable us to give it a go. We isolated the engine air filters, to gain a little more power and I did the first take off. I managed to unstick OK just before the soft bit so the rest followed me. We had decided that we would make the trip a bit more useful than just a ferry flight, so we didn't tell Deversoir that we were coming and on arrival we attacked the airfield with a series of co-ordinated, dummy rocket and bomb attacks. This showed up a number of weaknesses in our air defence scheme and it was hastily rewritten. The first Arab-Israeli war was just about to start and we had no idea if the politicians would get us involved. So we prepared ourselves 'just in case'.

In spite of, or maybe because of, the politicians, we did get involved and, on 22 November 1948, as a dress rehearsal for the real thing, we had a wing 'Balbo' down the Red Sea. A 'Balbo' is so called after the Italian general Balbo (who led a large formation of Italian flying boats on a trip across the Atlantic before the Second World War). In our case, both 6 and 213 Squadrons were involved. The station commander led such formations and I flew as his number two. The aircraft were all armed with eight 60-pound rockets and full ammunition for the 20-millimetre cannon. We went down the Red Sea at very low level – about 50 feet for about 150 miles – and then the wing carried out a series of attacks on some simulated targets near the coast. After totally destroying the 'enemy' we formed up to return to the Canal Zone, still at 50 feet. After some 15 minutes, I thought I heard a call on the radio. No one else seemed to have noticed it so I told the formation leader that I thought base was calling. He instructed me to pull up and see what they wanted so I climbed to about 500 feet above the sea and gave them a call. They replied with the information that the weather was deteriorating rapidly with a severe sandstorm and they advised an immediate recovery back to base. This information was passed on to the formation leader who made a totally original and long to be remembered call: 'Every man for himself, go, go, go.' Some 30 throttles were pushed fully forward and all the aircraft accelerated to their maximum speed. Sure enough when we got back to the Zone, the visibility below about 2000 feet was down to around 50 yards. Since the aircraft in those days carried nothing in the way of avionic navigation aids we were all rather poorly placed. Around 30 Tempests started milling around the Canal Zone in the middle of the sandstorm looking for somewhere to land. Not my idea of fun. I managed to catch sight of the threshold of one of the runways at an airfield near ours so a very rapid turn, a quick lowering of the undercarriage and flaps, followed by a call to Fayid Tower that I was about to land on Runway 24 (I think it was). This provoked a call from another Tempest pilot, 'I'm landing on Runway 06.' This threw me a bit, but not to be beaten, I came out with the call, 'OK you keep right, I'll keep left… As you were, let's both keep right!' Anyhow, very shortly, I was on the ground and so was he. On the opposite end of the same runway that I was on. I kept my aircraft close to the right-hand edge of the runway, which I could just see, and eventually I reached the other end. So did the other guy. Neither of us saw the other at any time, but the runway was wide enough – fortunately. Every pilot in the Wing managed to get his aircraft down safely somewhere but we were spread over the six or so airfields in the Canal Zone.

Some two months later, on 7 January 1949, my aircraft had been used in the morning by another pilot for an escort job and for that it had been fully armed. Since there was a war in progress between Egypt and Israel, for some flights we were armed and on others, we were not. The aircraft always carried full ammunition tanks, but when 'unarmed' the mechanism to feed the ammunition to the guns was removed. This was a bit of kit called a BFM or Belt Feed Mechanism. If these were fitted, a card was hung on the control column saying 'Guns cocked – ready to fire'. On this particular day, the Wing was stood down for the afternoon and we all retired to the Mess for lunch followed by a bit of recreation. In my case that meant working on an air-sea rescue boat which we had salvaged and were trying to get seaworthy again. Not long after lunch, the Tannoy burst into life, recalling all personnel and instructing the Wing to scramble. I stopped a passing Army lorry and told the driver to give me a ride up to the Flight Line, where I grabbed my helmet and parachute and ran to my aircraft. I pulled the chocks away, the ground crew having not arrived there yet, scrambled up to the cockpit, opened the canopy, got in, chucked out the card saying 'guns cocked – ready to fire,' pressed the primer pump motor, and fired a starter cartridge. The engine burst into life so, releasing the brakes, I rolled towards the runway and caught up with the station commander who was my 'number one' on such occasions. My own 'number two' went as spare man for the squadron, and in fact he ended up in one of the empty slots, where a pilot had been off base when the alert went off and so couldn't take his own place. We got airborne, still doing up our harness and settling into the routine. The Wing climbed in a battle formation to around 10,000 feet. What most of us didn't know at the time, was that a formation of four Spitfires from another airfield had gone out in the morning for a reconnaissance of the battlefield area and none of them had returned. Our primary task was to try and find out what had happened to them. In fact, all four had been shot down. The first one, flown by a friend of mine, F/Sgt Frank Close, had been hit by ground fire, forcing the pilot to bail out and the other three were shot down by Israeli fighters. The Israeli Air Force had both Me 109s and Spitfires while the Egyptian Air Force had also got Spitfires and some Macchi 202 aircraft which look very like the Me 109. So identification of friend from foe was not easy, to say the least. Anyhow, we proceeded towards the area where the Spitfires had vanished and as we approached the nominal border with Israel, we were attacked by the Israeli Air Force. Sadly, my own number two, Pilot Officer David Tattersfield, was hit in the first attack and was killed when his aircraft crashed in the desert. In my own case, I found myself head on to a Me 109 who was happily shooting at me. Flicking the safety catch to fire I pressed my trigger but to my dismay, nothing happened. The only thing that entered my head was that, like an idiot, I had forgotten to turn something on, so my hand flashed round the cockpit and the best I could do was put the navigation lights on. The Me 109 pilot was not over frightened by this. He broke over the top of me so I turned hard, to try and get behind him, while I sorted out why my guns would not fire. I found a Spitfire on my tail who was firing happily (and hitting me) so I jettisoned my drop tanks (which almost hit him) and took fairly violent evasive action. I gather that I was reported by the Israeli pilot of the Spitfire as 'last seen losing height rapidly with smoke pouring from the engine.' This was correct but the smoke was due to my over-boosting the engine and I was losing height because, although the Spitfire could out turn me, my aircraft was quite a lot faster and I needed that speed. The official Israeli Air Force report claimed me as a 'probable'. I'm delighted that this was an over assessment. In due course, I joined up with the station commander again and when the skies had cleared, we went home. I still have a bullet which was removed from the armour plate behind the seat. Incidentally, I have since met two of the Israeli guys who were there that day. One of them had an entry in his logbook stating that he had shot down an RAF aircraft. Sadly, I was able to countersign the entry confirming his claim. The second Israeli pilot was on the same Weapons Instructor Course as I was, at the RAF Central Gunnery School at Leconfield in Yorkshire in 1951. It's a small world in aviation. The reason why my guns would not fire was because, the Wing having been stood down, the armourers decided to service all the BFMs and had taken them out, intending to replace them later, but had left the cards in the cockpits.

Not long after the Wing was detached to Deversoir, on

the north edge of the Great Bitter Lake, I was put in charge of the sailing club. We didn't have many boats nor did we have much enthusiasm. What we did have was one of the old wartime Mark 2 Airborne Lifeboats. This had a wooden hull, designed I believe by Uffa Fox, which in operational form was dropped from an aircraft, usually a Wellington, to survivors in a life raft. At bow and stern it had automatically inflating flexible rubber flotation bags which made it self righting. It was fitted with a mast and sail, both pretty small and it had a marine version of the Austin 10 engine. There were numerous waterproof lockers in the hull which contained a variety of 'goodies', intended to enable crashed aircrew to stay alive. Our version had no inflatable bags and the engine was a bit tatty, to say the least, so it was removed and put into an empty hut near the Sergeants' Mess. Here it was worked on by a few keen volunteers and by the end of our first winter at Deversoir it had been completely overhauled and re-installed in the boat. Eventually the great day came for a 'test flight'. To our amazement it worked well and the boat chugged around at a fair rate of knots. There were one or two minor adjustments needed and we decided to take it for a longer run the following day. In due course a friend and I set out, and went some miles out into the Great Bitter Lake. We both had a swim in the much cleaner water away from the coast and set off home. Our route took us past a flotilla of some 15 fishing boats which were based in the bay next to the sailing club. The wind had vanished and, as a result, the becalmed boats were being sculled very slowly homewards. So, being a kind chap, I tied a long rope to a strong point on the stern of the lifeboat and took a slow orbit round the fishing boats. The crews got the idea and all tied their boats to the rope and we set off for home. With 15 boats to tow we were only making slow progress – indeed very little faster than they were being sculled – but with a great deal less effort. I took the boats right into their bay and they slipped the tow at appropriate moments, to run gently ashore while I returned to the sailing club jetty. I moored the lifeboat and, when I had made everything secure, made my way to the club house. There on the step was a large basket of prawns, many of which were still alive and so obviously very fresh. They made a nice addition to the supper in the Mess that evening. Strangely, we hardly ever had any kit stolen from the club after that.

One Saturday five guys and I set off from Deversoir in the airborne lifeboat on a long haul across the Great Bitter Lake towards Fayid. We had been offered an old Fairmile launch as a club house and we wanted to see what needed doing to it to make it sea worthy so that we could tow it back. The wind was fresh to strong, right in our faces and the boat could only make about 7 or 8 knots. The temperature was bitterly cold and I for one was wearing three sweaters under my waterproof jacket. We all huddled in the stern keeping out of the wind as best we could. Suddenly we noticed that we had a problem. The bows were awash. Hurriedly cutting the engine to a tick over, we started to bail frantically but within another two minutes the boat simply sank under us. A motley selection of debris came to the surface including some empty jerry-cans. These we collected and tied together. It was several miles into wind to get to Fayid and just about as far down wind to get back to Deversoir so we slowly paddled down wind. About an hour after we were due at Fayid, the guy who had gone round by road was getting concerned as he couldn't even see us in the distance. So he phoned Deversoir to see if we were going to come. He was told that we left three hours ago on what should have been a two-hour trip. Fortunately he had his head screwed on properly and he instigated a search party. A boat belonging to the Suez Canal Company was found at the Canal Station, where the Suez Canal enters the Bitter Lakes and this set off along our probable track. Meanwhile, we were beginning to suffer from hypothermia so I decided to take one of the jerry-cans and set off to try to get assistance for the others who were in a worse condition than I was. After what seemed like an age, I spotted the outbound searching boat and violent splashing attracted its attention. I told them where the others were and not to wait for me. They chucked me a life belt and went on to where the others were floating and drifting about a mile behind me. They were all picked up and taken at full speed to the Canal Station where several ambulances had been waiting for us. Meanwhile I continued to drift and I was beginning to wonder if they had forgotten me when I saw a rowing boat coming towards me. The two RAF guys in it hauled me over the stern and set off back to the Canal where I was transferred to an ambulance and then taken to join the others in the Station Sick Quarters. Slowly, very slowly, we thawed out, aided by a large urn of sweet tea. I was surprised by how many visitors we had – each of whom was given a cuppa – but I realised why when I was able to taste the 'additives' which had been slipped into the urn by our 'friends' Needless to say, we were kept in for 'observation' for a few days and then three of us were found to have hepatitis and three had pleurisy or pneumonia. Naturally I had hepatitis and pleurisy together. Indeed I was quite ill and what was worse I was off alcohol for 12 months when I eventually recovered.

Not long after that extended swim and its consequences, I was tour-expired and they shipped me back to the UK for yet another period of 14 days' leave. At the end of my leave I was told to report to Great Massingham just outside Norwich. Here I was employed in the Operations Room while they decided what to do with me.

3

Jets: 1949–54

When I returned from the Middle East in the middle of May of 1949, I was attached to RAF Great Massingham, a fighter station just outside Norwich. A few weeks after I arrived there, the RAF held its annual 'War' with itself. Bomber Command used to attack the UK and Fighter Command defended it. The Massingham Wing was deployed to RAF Finningley, near Doncaster, and I went with them as part of their Operations Room staff. On day one, the attacking aircraft, Hornets, Mosquitoes and Lancasters, had been making successful strikes against fighter airfields and, early on day two, as a direct result of these air attacks, I received a phone call from the Finningley Station Commander telling me that he had been authorised to scramble up to two aircraft on local airfield defence. He also said that he was delegating that authority to us in the Ops room, since we were the only people who knew what was going on. All the crews were briefed accordingly. Having a spare moment, I decided to phone around the local Army units and I asked them to let me know, urgently, if they saw any aircraft, and which way the aircraft were going. The intention was to use them as a sort of private Observer Corps of my own. They were happy to provide this service. At about 12.15 that day, most of the Ops Room staff went for a meal, leaving me and a couple of airmen to man the fort in the operations room. At about 12.25 the phone rang and a semi-hysterical voice told me that there were 'hundreds of aircraft heading my way at low level'. Pausing only to pick up a box of cartridges, went to the door and fired a 'Red Very' – to scramble two aircraft on local airfield defence, and then another to scramble two more, and another and another and another until eventually all 24 Meteor fighters were airborne. As the last two climbed away, there was a mighty roar and a motley formation of Lancaster bombers started an attack on our airfield. The Meteors had a field day, there were aircraft wheeling and diving in all directions. Why none of them collided I will never know, but there was a panic call from the station commander wanting to know what the heck was going on. I explained that the airfield was under attack from some 20-plus Lancasters and he had just scrambled all 24 aircraft on local airfield defence. 'I can't do that,' he said. 'I can only scramble two aircraft.'

'It's OK, sir, they were scrambled two at a time,' I replied.

Seconds later, the sector controller phoned to tell us that the last 'hostile' aircraft had just headed out to sea and we could stand everyone down for an hour as there were no enemy forces over the UK. He was a bit shaken when I described what was going on over our airfield. The Air Defence Radar had failed to pick the formation up when it had crossed the coast and nobody knew they were there. Apart from my private Observer Corps, that is. Just for once, I seemed to be popular with everyone (except the Lancaster crews).

In due course the Air Force decided to send me to RAF Acklington in Northumberland. This airfield was an Armament Practice Camp and was located just outside Morpeth. My job was to fly one of the Martinets, towing a target for the squadron pilots to shoot at. This was not the world's most exciting job, except when the pilots firing at my target, held their fingers on the trigger a bit too long and I could hear the shells going past my aircraft. None of them actually hit me but when you can hear the crack of a shell passing you, above the noise of the engine, then it's a bit closer than I like. Only two interesting things happened to me there. The first was when I was towing a target just off the coast and the engine stopped. I told my winch operator to jettison and he didn't hesitate. Some 4000 yards of steel cable went out the back with a high pitched scream and a smell of overheated winch. Meanwhile I turned hard left and to my surprise not to mention pleasure, I saw a disused airfield in front of me. I had just enough height to reach one of the runways and we landed safely with no damage to anything or anyone. I sent the winch man to find a telephone and told him to ring Acklington and tell them that we had force landed at Boulmer airfield and could they organise some transport. He came back about 15 minutes later and a few minutes behind him another aircraft arrived and landed alongside me. In it was our chief engineer. He checked the obvious things and managed to start the engine. He told me that he thought it was probably an airlock in the fuel system, and asked me if I was prepared to fly it back to Acklington if he volunteered to come in the back seat. It seemed like a good suggestion and so we took off and returned uneventfully. My own winch man came back in the other aircraft.

The second item of interest was when I was sent down to Group Headquarters to see the Air Officer Commanding the Group. I borrowed an aircraft and flew to RAF Newton, near Nottingham, and went in to see him. He asked what seemed to be the usual routine questions and then told me to go back to Acklington. Here, a couple of days later, I was sent for by the Station Commander who sat me down and said that the Air Force had decided to give me a Short Service Commission. I rather took him aback when I said that I was grateful, but I didn't want one. I explained that I was already 22 years old and after an eight-year commission I would be thirty, and would have to compete with guys who were ten years younger than me. I told him that when I left the Air Force in a few weeks, I intended going back to college to get a degree and then look for employment while I was still young enough to have a chance of getting a job. He took my point and I left the Air Force a few weeks later when my three-year engagement was up. I was sorry to go. I had flown some of the most exciting pieces of machinery ever invented, in the form of single-seat fighter aircraft, and I had been to some fascinating places. So I went back to college. I started with a specialist crammer in Godalming where I revised all I had forgotten since leaving school in 1942 and then in nine months I completed a three-year course of Pure Mathematics, Applied Mathematics, Physics and Chemistry. In the evenings I would travel home in a complete daze with my brain absolutely saturated with new learning. Then, unexpectedly, I got a letter from the Air Ministry which offered me a permanent commission in the Royal Air Force. I didn't need a second letter. There were all the usual selection boards to go through but having done seven years in the Air Force, I was well placed to impress them.

Having been recalled to full duty, I was soon sent to RAF Bircham Newton in Norfolk to be taught 'how to be an officer'. During part of this training we were involved in our own private 'war games' with other groups of young potential officers. Amongst other things, the directing staff were trying to teach us a modicum of military training and on this occasion, the two Courses at Bircham Newton went out for a two-day exercise in the field. Naturally there was considerable rivalry between the Courses and each side was determined to get one up on its opponents. After a period of cross-country movement, my side had to dig in at the edge of an airfield and, surprise surprise, the other side were digging in on the opposite edge of the airfield. At about 4 pm, I was called over by our Course Commander and detailed to organise a patrol. Our task was to reconnoitre the 'enemy' installation in preparation for a dawn attack the next morning and if possible to take a prisoner. I was also directed by our head umpire to bring back with me the cap of one of the opposing side's umpires. I decided that speed was the prime requirement so I selected a particularly agile group of four fit and healthy officer cadets and we set off on a roundabout route towards the other side of the airfield. The first interruption came when we were passing a stone quarry. We heard movement ahead so, concealing ourselves, we watched a guy, who was nothing to do with our exercise, creep along the path to the quarry. He looked highly suspicious and we watched while he went over to a wood and corrugated iron hut, where he proceeded to force the door and go inside. About two minutes later he came out, shut the door and came back down the track.

We decided that he was up to no good so, when he came abeam our position, we jumped him and, I think the word is, 'restrained' him. Naturally using minimum force. He went as white as a sheet and told us for God's sake to take care, or we would blow ourselves up. A little bit of prompting and a search showed that he had several sticks of gelignite in two of his pockets and some detonators in another pocket. This left us a bit nonplussed. After discussion we decided to march him down to the local village and let the village policeman look after him. So we all duly arrived on the policeman's doorstep and handed him over, informing the poor local bobby that the 'prisoner' was carrying gelignite and detonators. We then left. We now had to hurry, arriving in the vicinity of the rear of the 'enemy' position just as it was getting dark at about 21.30 hours. We took cover in some bushes. Shortly after pub closing time, of 22.00 hours, we heard some guys coming from the village. They turned out to be the opposition's umpires and one of the more enterprising cadets from the opposition. This was too good an opportunity to miss. We leaped out of the bush and grabbed the poor harmless (and full of beer) cadet. We managed to knock two of the umpires over in the mêlée and, grabbing one of their hats, we set off at high speed across the airfield, taking the most direct route home and frog-marching our prisoner with us. Arriving at the other side, I saw some movement and we all dropped to the ground. A careful look established that there was an 'enemy' patrol just in front of our lines. I thought about this and decided on a giant bluff. I was sure the enemy patrol knew we were there but didn't want to disturb our defences, so telling the others in a stage whisper to wait while I went and gave the password, I got to my feet and walked boldly towards our positions. Inevitably, I was challenged in the appropriate manner and I announced that I was 'friend' rather than 'foe'. When told to advance and give the password which was 'Stafford Cripps', I stepped forward and in a clear voice said 'General Montgomery' following it with a whisper of 'keep silent'. Fortunately they did and I got close enough to whisper to them that there was a 'hostile patrol' just outside our perimeter. They cottoned on and so I called to the rest of my patrol: 'Come on quickly chaps, the other patrol will be along in a few minutes and they have just had a brew up here.'

My team immediately came in and we waited. Sure enough, as expected, the 'enemy' had heard the password and advanced in a group. When challenged they were told to send one person forward to give the password. One unsus-pecting guy came forward and said 'General Montgomery'. He was promptly silenced and the next guy told to come forward. And the same thing happened. And the next guy and then the next. We now had five prisoners and one umpire's hat. Everyone was delighted that we had wiped the smile off the face of the other Course. They even had the nerve to ask for their guys back 'as it made the sides so uneven'. 'You must be joking,' was the approximate reply we gave them.

Having completed the Officer Training Course, I was returned to flying and went to RAF Finningley in Yorkshire for a flying refresher course and for conversion on to jet fighters. Here I once more flew the Harvard and as soon as I had got my hand in again I was converted to flying the Meteor VII, a two-seat twin engine jet trainer version of the single seat fighter.

Shortly after receiving my Commission, I decided to buy a car and after much hunting I found a 1932, F type MG. This car was a four-seat 'tourer' with a six-cylinder, single-overhead camshaft engine. Over the years I slowly rebuilt it bit by bit. It hardly ever let me down but on one occasion it tried to. I had been out somewhere and when I set off home at about 10 pm, I had travelled only a couple of miles when there was a twang of some sort and I found the clutch cable had broken and I was stuck with no ability to de-clutch. The roads were pretty empty so I continued slowly and carefully, changing gear without de-clutching – it was a straight-toothed, 'crash' gearbox – and I was making good progress until I got to Doncaster. Here I noticed the traffic light ahead was red so I slowed and slowed and slowed. Eventually I crawled towards the lights in first gear at all of three miles per hour while I waited for the lights to change. They never change when you want them to and these were no exception. As I reached them I could see that there were no vehicles anywhere in any direction so I crossed – on the red. It was not my day, and sure enough the local bobby stepped out of a doorway and raised his hand. I stopped and the expected conversation ensued. Yes, I had seen the lights, No, I had not stopped. Yes, I did have my licence with me. I then explained that once stopped I had no means of getting started again, hence the 'failure to stop'. He was definitely a gentleman because he accepted my explanation. What's more I even prevailed upon him to push me down the road so that I could get into gear again! I got back to camp with no more difficulty and sorted out the broken clutch cable in the morning. That car had a distressing habit of blowing cylinder-head gaskets but this happened so often that I got the time down to 20 minutes to change the gasket on the roadside. And remember this was an engine with an over-head camshaft so it had to be re-timed each time. I carried a stack of gaskets and a jerry can full of water with me, plus a set of special spanners so that I could work on the cylinder-head studs without removing the rockers. I finally sold the car for about three times what I had paid for it, but by then I had had the block scraped flat and new cylinder-head studs fitted so it had stopped blowing gaskets.

In February 1951, I was sent to Driffield in Yorkshire to learn to fly the Vampire, one of the first of the jet fighters. While I was here, I did my dual flying in the Meteor VII because it was the only two-seat jet aircraft, and my solo flying in the Vampire single-seat fighter. My instructor (Flt Lt Pete Marman) was also the instructor detailed to fly the prototype two-seat Vampire which was at Driffield at that time, on trials for the Service. This aircraft (registered as G 57 P) was essentially still the property of the De Havilland Aircraft Company and the crew consisted of an observer from the company plus my instructor. One cold day in March my instructor walked into the bar and announced that he would allow anyone who wanted to, to buy him a drink as he was now the most experienced pilot in the world on type. When the inevitable challenge was offered to this claim, he pointed out that the aircraft was the only one of its type in the world, it had just gone back to De Havilland's for its first 50-hour check and he had 28 hours as pilot-in-command on it. There was no answer to this, so I can safely say that I was trained in part by the world's most ex-perienced pilot.

Having completed my conversion training, I went, with several other pilots, to Chivenor in Devon to learn the operational techniques of flying jet fighters. This included lots of formation flying and general handling and we were also taught to use the aircraft as a weapons platform. The aircraft had four 20 millimetre cannons and could be fitted with either two bombs of up to 1,000 lb each or with 8 three-inch, 60-pound rockets. We were also taught the rudiments of air combat and at the end of this rather enjoyable course I was posted to Hong Kong. This was a wonderful place for a young officer to go. You would never believe the prices we were asked for things. On the flying side there are a few memories to tell you about. The first one that springs to mind was the time I was detailed to take a formation of four aircraft and carry out rocket attacks on a target towed by HMS *Belfast*. The ship was en route to Hong Kong and it was a good chance to get some training on 'ship' targets. Each aircraft carried eight 60-pound rockets, and these we fired in pairs at the splash target which was towed about 800 yards behind the cruiser. Having expended our live rockets, the briefed drill was that we would then carry out co-ordinated practice attacks on the ship, which would oppose us with its full armament, firing bakelite break-up shot. These were the right diameter but disintegrated to dust on leaving the gun and so should do no damage, but they produce sufficient recoil to operate the automatic weapons. Before we could start these attacks, the ship, understandably, insisted that we each flew past slowly at low level so that they could confirm that all our rockets had been fired, and that we carried no ordnance which could cause them any damage. This was no problem and after their inspection we broke away and started our attacks. It was great fun; we came in very low and very fast from both sides at once and the ship had a terrific time firing away with everything they had. Clouds of brown smoke, lots of noise, and great fun was had by all. Eventually we got down to 'bingo fuel' so the time had come to return home. We formed up, flew over the ship in a farewell salute and set off towards home. In the fullness of time we landed normally, and after parking my aircraft I went into the crew room to be told that there was a call for me on the phone. When I asked who it was, the answer, by the squadron joker, was 'Oh, its only the Commander-in-Chief.' So I picked up the phone and was a bit thunderstruck to find that it was indeed the Commander-in-Chief.

'I just wanted to ring and give you my personal apology,' he said. 'I can assure you that that officer's feet won't touch the ground for a long time.'

'Er, I seem to have missed something, sir,' I replied. 'What are you talking about?'

'Weren't you the officer leading that formation of aircraft working with *Belfast*?' he asked.

'Yes, sir,' I replied.

'How much damage did they do?' was the next question.

'None that I know of,' I answered.

'I'll have them for that too then,' he replied. 'Didn't they tell you that they were using the wrong ammunition? Apparently they used contact break-up ammunition which we use against ship targets not aircraft.'

I was a bit nonplussed. If I had known they were firing solid shot I wouldn't have gone within miles of them unless I still had had some of my rockets on board. But, I'm glad they were rotten shots for once. But I don't think the Commander-in-Chief was so pleased that they had missed us all.

Somewhere about that time, the squadron had arranged to do an Escape and Evasion exercise with the RAF Regiment. On the day in question, we were taken by sea to an isolated peninsula somewhere north-east of Kowloon and we were required to try and get back to the airfield at Kai Tak. Another pilot, called Bill Honey, and I had paired up and, using our extensive knowledge of the local terrain which we had gained on various reconnaissances of the area, we decided to travel light. We wore light plimsolls and carried the minimum of equipment. The defensive forces were due to be deployed at 16.00 hours and we reckoned that we might well get most if not all of the way back to the 'safe line' before they deployed, if we could travel fast enough. So we set off at very high speed and indeed our calculations were correct. We would have 'got safe' before 16.00 hours, but at 15.30 hours we spotted the regiment guys deploying early and so the best laid plans of mice and men ... Switch to Plan B. This involved lying up in a ditch until it was dark and then working our way up a steep scree and lowering ourselves down a small cliff on to the safe area. This was grand until Bill started to suffer from heat exhaustion as a result of all our exertions running hard in the early stages of the exercise. I gave him all the water we had and did a reconnaissance of the last 100 yards. The defenders seemed to be leaving that part of the hill alone so, having collected Bill, we very slowly worked our way to the top of the cliff. Here we found that a shortage of equipment for the descent made life very difficult, but by cutting several branches from some tall shrubs and tying them together we managed to get a 'rope', which I hoped would be long enough. I tied Bill at the top of the cliff, armed with a knife, and worked my way down the 'rope'. It was nearly long enough, I only had about five feet to drop. Having told Bill to follow, he cut the line lashing him to the top of the cliff and followed me down successfully. By good fortune there was a cattle drinking trough about 100 yards up the road, so we went up there and I immersed Bill in the trough. This cooled him down and also enabled him to rehydrate to some degree. Just then we heard a vehicle coming and so ducked down into the ditch at the side of the road. Even if we were on the so-called 'safe road', I was taking no chances. The vehicle passed us and I recognised it as an RAF staff car. After stopping about 200 yards down the road, the car turned round, came back up the hill, passed us and went on to a track about 25 yards up the hill from us which we had not noticed. It stopped, the door opened, the driver got out and walked into the scrub area. Being nosy, we investigated and we discovered that it was the Station Commander's car and he was visiting one of the RAF Regiment posts about 30 yards down the track. We also noticed that he had left the keys in the ignition. Never being ones to look a gift horse in the mouth, we climbed in, released the brake, rolled back on to the road, started the engine and quietly drove off. It was no great distance back to Kai Tak, so we parked the vehicle carefully in the CO's parking slot and, like well trained pilots, went into the bar. Needless to say, we were filthy, Bill was still wet and I have no doubt we were a bit smelly. Anyhow the other officers in the bar all moved away to the other end of the bar and we settled down to a bit of rehydration. Some 15 minutes later an RAF Regiment jeep drew up with a scattering of gravel. There was a pause and a somewhat peeved-looking Station Commander came into the bar. He was pretty quick on the uptake. One look at Bill and me, and a slow grin settled over his face.

'OK you two, I might have guessed it was you Rufus. I suppose it serves me right for leaving it unlocked with the keys in it.'

'That's right, sir,' I replied, 'and the drinks are on you.'

He didn't seem to object to the dirt, wet or smell, when he joined us: and sure enough the drinks were on him . . .

Some ten years after I thought I had finished flying Harvards, I was in Singapore and needed to get from RAF Seletar to RAF Changi. It was only a few miles but trying to organise a vehicle was tedious in the extreme so I asked if I could borrow the station Harvard and fly over. This was approved, so shortly after, I duly set off, accompanied by one of the airmen who also wanted to get to Changi for some reason or other. The main thing I remembered about the Harvard was its landing speed of 65 over the hedge. So, in the fullness of time, I set myself up for the landing and progressively reduced speed until I crossed the hedge at 65. I was surprised to find how 'twitchy' the Harvard was after the Vampires and Meteors which I had been flying recently and I was amazed at the shortness of the landing run. We taxied in, parked and I went about my business. About two hours later I returned to the aircraft and since the airman was not yet there I sat down in the cockpit and idly looked at the instruments. That was when the penny dropped. That particular aircraft had its air speed indicator calibrated in miles per hour. Normally they were calibrated in knots. This made a difference of eight and a half miles per hour and accounted for the unstable handling and the remarkably short ground run. Our return flight and subsequent landing at Seletar were models of accuracy. I certainly learnt the lesson that you can't take anything for granted in connection with aeroplanes.

Later, while I was still at Seletar there was an incident which had both its funny and its unfortunate sides. The Medical Officer was a young, fairly recently qualified, doctor and he was determined to make a name for himself. One lunchtime, an aircraft crashed on landing and the aircraft concerned came to rest off the runway in one of the vast monsoon ditches which surrounded everything in the Far East. The MO rushed to the ambulance as soon as the crash bell sounded and he and the driver sped off to the rescue. Arriving first at the scene, he jumped out, saw that the aircraft crew were still in the aircraft and with no more ado, jumped down into the monsoon ditch – and broke both his legs. The aircraft crew then climbed out of the aircraft. Their only injury was to their pride. They assisted the ambulance driver down into the ditch, with a stretcher, and between them they lifted the doctor into his own ambulance and carried him off to the Station Sick Quarters where his legs were dealt with. Somehow I don't think that was quite the way in which the MO wanted to get known.

During my tour in Hong Kong, I was sent on a Weapons Instructor Course at Leconfield in Yorkshire so I will include the next memory even if it relates to a Meteor rather than a Vampire. About half-way through the course, I was on the air to ground rocket range in a Meteor VIII. This is the single-seat, ground-attack/fighter version. I had fired about half of the eight rockets I was carrying and as I came round for my fifth attack, I was called by the range officer and told that base had been on the phone and they wanted me back as soon as possible, or sooner. Turning my attack into a ripple of all my remaining rockets, I opened the taps and headed for home. The aircraft was light and had no ventral tank to slow it down so it was nicely wound up when I arrived. The runway was approximately lined up with my approach and having done a shallow dive for the last five miles, I passed over the runway threshold at well over 600 knots and at a very low level. I popped the dive brakes out, retarded the throttles and entered a climbing turn at +6G. My speed decayed rapidly and, following a very tight circuit, I was able to retract the dive brakes, lower the undercarriage and the flaps and come in over the hedge at the correct speed. I dropped it on the ground right at the start of the runway and braked very hard. I was down to about 30 knots, when I went into a wall of rapidly advancing snowflakes. Visibility was cut to about ten yards and I had great difficulty finding my way back to the dispersal. Had I returned in a more sedate manner, I would have had to divert. And the nearest airfield was a long way south and already had rapidly deteriorating conditions. I doubt if I'd have got there before they went out.

The next little bit of excitement was on 17 October 1951 when I was airborne on an unusually cloudy day for Hong Kong. I'd taken off from the small airfield at Sek Kong in the New Territories with the intention of doing some general handling and aerobatics at about 20,000 feet. I had noticed that the cloud base was around 1,500 feet and I remembered that the mountain of Timo Shan just to the east of the airfield went up to about 3,500 feet. As I passed

Vampire V at Kai Tak: 1951

16,000 feet there was an almighty bang and the aircraft rotated rapidly. My first thought was that a wing had come off, however fortunately the rolling stopped and I took stock of the situation. It was eerily quiet. The engine was reading Zero RPM so I set the aircraft into a glide and thought about what to do. The alternatives seemed to be: to bail out, or to stay with it and try to force land somewhere. I soon rejected Plan A as the Vampire is not the best of aircraft to bail out from, because the pilot usually hits the tail. The aircraft has to be inverted anyhow and I didn't fancy that option very much. Added to this, the South China Sea is full of unpleasant things like sharks and pirates and it would be just my luck to come across both. So I decided to do a forced landing. My Mayday distress call had been ignored so I repeated it. This time the only reaction I got was an acknowledgement. Trying to remember my track since I took off, I worked out where Kai Tak airfield ought to be and went for it. As I passed the area safety height of 5,500 feet, I thought I had been a bit stupid not to have bailed out, but my luck was in and I broke cloud at 1,500 feet exactly where I hoped to be – over the harbour. Adjusting my flight path to land on the runway which points straight at Lion Rock (remember this is the old Kai Tak with only two short runways. The long runway out into the harbour wasn't started until 1955). I had judged it quite well for once and when I was sure that I would make the airfield, I selected, Wheels down, Flaps down and Airbrakes out. And absolutely nothing happened. What I didn't know was that the bang as the engine broke up had destroyed my hydraulic system and there is no pressure gauge in the cockpit. This meant that I was very high and fast. I managed to force the aircraft on to the ground about 500 yards before the end of the runway, at very high speed. Realising that there was a nine-foot concrete fence at the end, and I was sitting in a balsa wood fuselage with a 96-gallon fuel tank behind me and a heavy jet engine behind that, I didn't feel like becoming the jam in the sandwich. With a flash of genius, I applied full aileron, dug my wing tip into the ground and managed to rotate the aircraft so that it was facing the other way when we hit the fence. That's where I seemed to lose control of the machine because it cartwheeled up the hill until the fuselage struck a building. We were just about sideways on to the house. The nose of the aircraft broke off and went on up the hill, leaving me strapped to the bulkhead with nothing in front or around me. I was not thinking very well at this stage – I had hit my head an almighty wallop on something hard, but I undid my straps, put my feet on the ground and walked (staggered?) away. I undid and dropped my parachute, and then thinking it seemed odd to have plants growing horizontally instead of vertically, I found myself lying on the ground. Shortly after this, the ambulance crew arrived, picked me up and carted me off to the Station Sick Quarters, where two nice kind PMRAFNSs cut all my clothes off and then carefully cut my helmet off and all my hair. The station MO managed to join up the split in my head and I was removed to bed, where I stayed for several days. The aircraft was a hell of a mess too.

About 14 days after that accident. I was once more allowed out. I was in the Officers' Club in Kowloon with one of our Air Traffic Controllers, Dave Routledge. We were about to start eating our meal when there was a piercing scream from a lovely young lady in the corner. The rest of the room went silent as she jumped to her feet and, loud and clear, said, 'Rufus darling, they told me you were dead!' She then ran across the room, flung her arms round me and burst into tears, amid the applause of the other diners. The guy who had taken her out to dinner was not very impressed but we persuaded them both to join us. It seems that she had been on the aircraft which had been delayed by my crash and the word that got out was that the pilot had been killed. I assured her that it was only a rumour.

The next bit of light relief was during the Korean conflict. We would periodically send the squadron up the coast, some ten miles out to sea. The visibility was excellent and the whole squadron would be there, usually at 35,000 feet. We could see the Chinese airfield at Swatow and when we were getting close, the airfield would go all hazy. That was the Mig 15s taking off to intercept us. So we would turn round and fly back down the coast to Hong Kong. On one such occasion we were flying up the coast as usual but this time nothing happened. This provoked some ribald remarks about the Chinese pilots being on a day off or on leave, when I happened to look up. There ahead of us, at about 45,000 feet was a squadron of Migs. I can assure you that we all did a very rapid about turn. The Mig was some 200 mph faster than us and just as manoeuvrable. It took the smug smiles off our faces.

Once upon a time... I was in an RAF Valetta en route

from Singapore to Hong Kong. The aircraft had night stopped at the USAF base at Clark Field in the Philippines and the next morning set off towards Hong Kong. On arriving at PNR (Point of No Return) we had been unable to raise Hong Kong on the W/T so in accordance with standing procedures we turned round and returned to Clark Field. The next day we tried again and this time we spoke to Hong Kong, but the weather was unfit so once more we returned to Clark Field.

The next day dawned bright and again, we set course for Hong Kong. Surely nothing could go wrong this time? Don't you believe it! Again we were unable to contact our destination so again we turned round to return. After some 20 minutes there was a buzz on the intercom. 'Hey Skipper, you know that head wind we had on the way here? Well, it's turned round and we have got a head wind on the way back. The trouble is we don't have enough fuel to get back to Clark Field.' That was the situation.

'Where's the nearest airfield?' came the reply.

'There is an emergency strip in the north-west corner of Luzon. That's the best bet. We should just have enough fuel to get there.'

So we headed for Laoag, the emergency strip. Sure enough we did have enough fuel to get there. The airfield had a runway made up of Pierced Steel Planking (PSP) and the grass was growing through the holes. Local cattle were grazing happily so a quick beat up to scatter them was the order of the day, followed by a fast, tight circuit to get on the ground before the cattle returned and before we ran out of fuel. In the fullness of time we arrived safely on the ground and taxied to the obvious parking area. There were no buildings, no aircraft and no people – not unlike the *Mary-Celeste* but without the half-eaten meal. Looking around the most deserted airfield I have ever seen, one of us spotted a column of dust and after a few minutes we could see the modified jeep producing the dust. The vehicle drew up alongside the aircraft and a short fat Filipino wearing the inevitable white suit got out.

'I'm sorry I was not here to meet you, gentlemen, but you are early,' he said. That had obviously lost something in the translation into English.

'Is it possible to get some fuel here?' we asked him.

'Oh yes that is all taken care of. My brother will be out later to refuel the aircraft but he had to go to market this morning and is not back yet,' he replied. Then his mouth opened and he looked at a bit of a loss for the first time since he had driven up. 'But there are seven of you,' he said, 'there should only be five. No worry,' he added, 'I will get some extra beds and there is plenty of food and drink.'

'Can you accommodate us overnight?' we asked.

'Of course, it has all been arranged as requested by the embassy in Manila. Our mouths opened in turn.

'What do you mean "as requested"?' we asked him. So with a broad smile he reached into his pocket and produced a letter a evidently written by the British Embassy in Manila some three weeks earlier, and he showed us that it asked him to meet an RAF Valetta which would land at Laoag at about 4 pm that day. It also asked him to arrange refuelling and to accommodate the crew overnight. All the bills were to be sent to the embassy.

So we had a relaxing meal and stayed overnight. The next morning after the usual greasy breakfast, our host drove us back to the aircraft, which was full of fuel, and we climbed aboard. This time we managed to contact Hong Kong and complete our journey.

I still wonder how the British Embassy in Manila knew that we would be forced to divert that day, into Laoag, and we would need food, bed, breakfast and petrol for the aircraft?

Our squadron (28 (F) Sqn) was based in the New

Territories and another RAF Squadron (No. 80 Sqn) was based at Kai Tak. They had Spitfires when I arrived in the Far East but after a while were re-equipped with Hornets. For those unfamiliar with the type, the Hornet is a single-seat aircraft rather like a Mosquito but much slimmer, considerably faster and was designed as a long-range fighter for the Far East war. The war ended before they could be used in anger, but they were a truly long-range high-performance aircraft. The Air Officer Commanding the RAF in Hong Kong was due for replacement and his successor decided that he would ferry one of the Hornets out to Hong Kong. The ferry trip was fairly uneventful until the leg from Singapore to Hong Kong. We were all standing by to escort him into the colony with a mass formation of 12 Vampires and 12 Spitfires. The weather gradually got worse and worse. Finally the AOC made a decision. Divert the AOC Designate to the USAF base at Clark Field in the Philippines. A message was duly passed, we were all told to land and a phone call was made to the Commanding Officer at Clark Field informing him of the diversion and the pilot's status. At Clark Field the general decided that, as the equivalent to a one-star general, our AOC Designate rated an escort, and so the duty pair of F80 jet fighters were scrambled to escort him into Clark Field. They were on the same radio frequency as the Hornet so the pilot was able to listen in.

'Hey Red two, it's only an old prop job, 80 per cent power should be enough.' The F 80s swung in a graceful arc behind the Hornet. Unabashed our AOC-to-be opened the throttle to max continuous.

'Hey Red two, it's faster than I thought, give it 98 per cent.' At once the Hornet pilot went to combat power and proceeded to pull away slowly.

'We got to catch this guy, Red two, give it 101 per cent – the general will crucify us if we aren't with him.'

The Hornet then entered a shallow dive, but slowly the

F80s closed on him. Quick as a flash, the pilot shut down and feathered one engine.

'Jeez, Red leader, what will those ships do on two engines?'

In due course they all three landed and while he taxied back, Air Traffic having noticed that our AOC had a shut-down engine, called him. 'Do you have a problem?' he was asked.

'No,' he replied. 'I just shut it down so that your boys could catch up.'

Another interesting day was when my Vampire had been unserviceable following a reported fuel leak. The engineers worked on it all morning and it was cleared to fly at about noon. I climbed in and took off intending to go up to around 30,000 feet and carry out some aerobatics and follow this with an instrument recovery and some circuits. The aircraft had been refuelled to full tanks before take off. As I passed about 22,000 feet in the climb, I looked at the fuel gauge to see it indicating that I had less than five minutes' fuel remaining. Panic! I closed the throttle put the airbrakes out and dived steeply to get up to the maximum permitted indicated airspeed of 455 knots which at 20.000 feet computes to about 615 knots true airspeed. I called the Tower at Sek Kong and told them that I was out of fuel and they cleared me to land. Turning to line up with the runway at about two miles' range, I was shocked to see that my very cold windscreen had frozen up and I could see 'the square root of nothing'. I asked the controller in the Tower to start firing Very lights and to tell me where they landed. He had a device like a revolver and so could fire them in pretty quick succession. Some overshot, some undershot, and some landed on the runway so I aimed my 'blind' aircraft at them. The touch down was hard (very) and I braked hard (very). The aircraft stopped, and after a bit of hard effort, I managed to open the canopy and see out. I was right on the very edge of the runway. I taxied slowly forward and parked on the apron. After getting out I told the flight sergeant engineer that I wanted the wheels removed and the brakes checked. About 30 minutes later, I went out to see the result and I was told that the port brake was perfect, no sign of overheating. I asked about the starboard one. I was told that they hadn't checked that one, there was no point. I insisted that they did check it, and I watched. As the wheel was removed, the brake sac fell out on to the tarmac as a pile of carbonised dust. The engineers were suitably abashed and the brake systems were both changed. What was even more maddening was the fact that the 'thump' of my landing had woken up the fuel gauge which was now reading three-quarters full.

The aircraft based in Hong Kong carried out a lot of weapons practice in order to keep our skills on the top line, ready for whatever might come up. Not only that, but it was great fun to attack harmless targets with 20-millimetre cannon or 60 lb rockets. On special occasions we also used 500 lb and 1,000 lb bombs but more often, we were limited to the 25 lb-smoke/flash practice bomb. The air to ground target consisted of an eight foot square wooden platform which had to be renewed at regular intervals and we also used this target for rocket attacks. The range officer sat in his brick hut which had a flat roof consisting, if I remember correctly, of asbestos sheets and he operated the radio and assessed the attacks. As Squadron Weapons Officer, it fell to my lot to be range officer quite frequently. On one occasion I was asked to act as range officer for the Spitfires of the Hong Kong Auxiliary Air Force who were scheduled to carry out rocket attacks followed by 20-millimetre strafing attacks. In due course I arrived at the range where I joined the rest of the range handling party and we inspected the target to make sure that it was OK and we also looked round the small peninsula on which the targets were positioned, to make absolutely certain that there was nobody trespassing in the range area. The first two Spitfires then arrived and, after completing a dummy attack first, they were cleared for live firing. The leader prepared for his first attack and as he rolled into the attack I remarked to the other members of the range party that it looked exactly as though he was lining up on the range officer's hut rather than on the target. As the aircraft continued its dive, I became more and more concerned about its evident flight path. Finally my nerve broke, I snatched up a Very pistol and fired a Red at right angles to his path. Too late. He had released his first two missiles so we stood there and watched the 'friendly fire' closing directly towards us at well over 750 mph. I had timed my Very pistol shot about right. The rockets had been fired out of range and fell some 150 yards short of my hut but directly in line with it. I was less than polite when I spoke to the pilot concerned. He in turn wanted to know what the hell I had been doing to clear him for a live attack when there were people 'standing by the target'. I explained, gently, that the target was 200 yards north of my hut and perhaps he would like to carry out another dummy attack? On the real target this time? It cost him more than one beer when we both got back to the Mess that evening before I finally forgave him.

The local fishermen who operated in the range area must have had a line to Air Headquarters, because when the last aircraft for the day had started its final attack, a fleet of fishing boats would set out at full speed to the area where the empty cartridge cases had been raining down during the firing runs. There the fishermen were over the side into the lovely clean water of Clear Water Bay and soon baskets of empty brass cases were being hauled up from the seabed, and carried off in triumph. I think we provided quite a contribution to the local salvage economy. When we had been using 500 or 1000 lb bombs, they were even quicker at going out to salvage the remains. The bombing target was in the sea and as you will imagine, there were plenty of dead fish everywhere. It was a lovely area which we had taken over as a gunnery range and at weekends, a friend of mine (Mike Clayton) and I used to get up there and do some fishing with face masks and home-made spear guns on our own account. That was in the 1950s. I have no doubt it has all changed now.

There was one occasion when Mike and I were out looking for fish when we each had home-made spear guns, operated by elastic. I had fired two or three shots, to no avail, and my 'spear' was getting a bit blunt. Mike called me over to where he was. As soon as I had joined him he led me slowly and carefully to where he could point out a large stingray lying on the bottom. Personally I considered our 'spears' too light for such a large fish but nothing daunted, Mile let fly. He missed by a very short measurement and then had the problem of how to retrieve his spear which was stuck in the sand about one inch from the fish's head. Against my better judgement I let him borrow my spear. Once more he took careful aim. This time it was an excellent shot and struck the fish between the eyes. Unfortunately being blunt it didn't penetrate. The fish was not amused. Very shortly after this débâcle, there were three lines of foam in Clear Water Bay. One was Mike, one was me and the other was the fish. I think we all got up to about the same speed but fortunately we all three took different directions. Later, when the sand had settled we returned to the spot and recovered both the spears. I still think it was a silly thing to have done.

One bright and sunny day one of our pilots (Mike Waudby) went off on a solo flight. He was detailed to climb to around 35,000 feet and carry our some general handling, followed by a practice instrument recovery. About 15 minutes into his flight, those of us who were sitting in the crew room heard a garbled noise on the radio. Quite evidently someone was in fairly serious trouble. We couldn't make out what he was saying but a bit of elimination soon established that it was Mike who had called. Air Traffic tried to raise him but to no avail. However a few minutes later a lone Vampire burst into the traffic pattern at Sek Kong and completed what I can best describe as a very 'untidy' circuit and landing. Indeed it was much more of an 'arrival' than a 'landing'. The aircraft taxied slowly up to the apron; stopped; and a remarkably 'different' Mike Waudby climbed out. He could hardly stand, he was as white as a sheet, he was shaking like the proverbial aspen leaf and obviously suffering from shock. We applied the usual restorative and after a few minutes he told us: he had decided to go on up to 40,000, where he levelled out and opened the throttle to do a high-speed run. (In those days there were no supersonic aircraft and the handling of aircraft at high Mach numbers left a lot to be desired.) As he approached M.0.8 he was looking down sun and the visibility was mainly glare with nothing solid for the eye to focus on. Being very high, sounds don't carry very well and the cockpit of a single-seat aircraft is a fairly lonely place. Suddenly he felt a couple of firm taps on his shoulder as though someone was trying to attract his attention. As Mike said, he nearly had a 'nasty anti-social accident'. He didn't dare look round in case he saw someone there with him, in the very small single-seat Vampire cockpit. He popped his air brakes out, throttled back and got down out of there as fast as he could. His pulse rate must have been well into the 200s and I'm not surprised that his landing was less than perfect. We went and looked at his aircraft. We found that the inner lamination of the canopy had cracked and under the turbulence of the high Mach number and the air blast of the pressurisation, the inner section could pivot down and 'tap him on the shoulder'. I'm glad it was him and not me that 'got the call'.

It was while I was visiting Kai Tak one weekend that I came across one of the Air Force's perennial line shooters in the Mess bar. He was buying drinks all round because he had that day achieved the distinction of totalling up '100 hours on type'. He was spouting forth to all and sundry about how he had celebrated with a display of aerobatics over the airfield but was firmly put in his place by an elderly aviator who raised his glass and said, 'Congratulations young man. As a matter of fact I passed the 3,000 hours on type last week myself.'

'Gosh!' said the youngster, 'I bet you really celebrated that didn't you?'

'Yes,' was the reply, 'I was a bit naughty, I descended 100 feet on the downwind leg.'

4

The UK: 1954–58

After returning to England from Hong Kong, I was posted to Stradishall in Suffolk. One day, I was tasked to fly a two-seat Vampire to Pembrey in South Wales to collect one of our Air Traffic Control Officers. All went well on the way to Wales and after refuelling, we set off on the return journey. The undercarriage wouldn't retract after take off, so I operated the over-ride switch and up it came. As we approached Stradishall, there was a heavy shower over the field and I was asked to delay my arrival while it had a chance to clear. In due course I joined the circuit and agreed to accept a five-knot tail wind as it was already five o'clock and everybody wanted to shut up shop for the day. I was slightly fast on the final part of my approach, so I popped the airbrakes out to get a bit more drag and on reaching the ground, I flared nicely. There was an agonising grinding noise from below and, thinking that I must have a flat tyre, I went around. The aircraft accelerated, I selected air brakes in, undercarriage up and flaps up. I called the Tower and told them that I thought that I had a flat tyre and requested a fly past for them to have a look at it. They reported that everything seemed to be as it should, and so I completed my circuit and landed. We taxied up to the hangar where a group of airmen grabbed the aircraft and pushed it inside. As I was getting out, I noticed one of the airmen bend down, look at the nose and snigger. Having removed my helmet, I looked at the underside of the nose and to my horror and surprise, I found the corner of the nose-wheel door had been ground off. Looking further I found that the bottom of the engine cowling was all scraped and the trailing edge of the flaps was damaged. I couldn't understand this but the following morning I had one of those one-way interviews with our OC Flying. It was the sort of interview where I stand smartly to attention and simply say, 'Yes, sir!' He ended up with the words, 'You are ruddy lucky you didn't write it off or you would have been looking at a court martial. Now get out.' Needless to say I got out, it was not the time to argue.

About a month later, I was flying the same aircraft, and when I taxied out with my second student he plugged his headset into the intercom socket in time to hear me completing my pre-take-off checks. Having been cleared to take off, I lined up on the runway, opened the throttle and got airborne. The aircraft was unusually sluggish and looking out I observed that the airbrakes were out. I retracted them and noticed that the student had observed my boob. 'That only goes to show,' I said, 'even instructors get it wrong some times.'

'Yes,' he said, 'and I heard you check them before take off. I'm surprised that the runway controller didn't stop you taking off with them out.'

'So am I,' I replied, 'but let's get on with the exercise.'

About half an hour later we rejoined the circuit to land. As I turned finals, there was an aircraft obstructing the runway and although there was room – just – I decided to go around. I applied full power, selected undercarriage up and there was an unusual trim change. Looking out, I found that the airbrakes were out. I gave the student a flea in his ear for putting them out, which he hotly denied, and so I instructed him to hold the selector lever in the 'in' position for the remainder of the sortie. After our next approach, we landed normally and I taxied back to the apron and parked. After getting out I snagged the aircraft with the entry 'Airbrakes coming out when undercarriage selected up.' This provoked several sarcastic remarks from the flight sergeant but I refused to alter it. Against the engineer's wishes, I insisted that they should jack the aircraft up and check it. About 15 minutes later, with the aircraft safely on jacks, the hydraulic test rig was connected and the Wing Commander Engineering Officer got in and told me to sit in the other seat. He then took hold of the undercarriage selector and selecting 'up' pointed to the lights which cycled normally and re-selecting down, pointed out to me that there was nothing wrong. Turning to the flight sergeant, he said, 'Nothing wrong with it is there Flight Sergeant?'

'No, sir,' was the reply, 'the airbrakes are fine, now try the undercarriage.'

The Wing Commander re-selected the undercarriage 'up' and out popped the airbrakes. He selected 'down' and in they went. There was a pregnant silence.

'I think I owe you an apology Rufus,' he said.

'I think you owe me two, sir,' I replied. 'This was the same aircraft that I was accused of trying to land with the wheels up last month. It's the same fault but the other way round. I put the airbrakes out last time and the wheels came up on their own.'

'I think you are right,' he said and, turning to the flight sergeant, he added, 'nobody is to touch it until De Havilland's get an engineer up here.'

Some while later the investigation was ended, and the Engineering Officer agreed that I had been blameless for the earlier incident. But OC Flying never mentioned it to me, from that day on.

Strangely enough, many years later when I working in the Ministry of Defence, I programmed the Flight Safety computer to select all Vampire landing and take-off accidents. After a final filter by hand, I ended up with four cards. The four cards consisted of my 'wheels up touch and go' and three accidents where a pilot had selected wheels 'up' immediately after take off and had then fallen out of the sky on to the ground and the aircraft had been written off. In each case the aircraft were found to have their airbrakes out and the pilots had each been given a formal 'reproof' 'for taking off with their airbrakes out', which had no doubt blighted their promotion prospects. I'm prepared to lay good odds that they had the same problem as I did, but I got away with it. There but for the grace of God . . .

During my time at Stradishall I was given the job of Officers' Mess Secretary. This was classed as a part-time job and involved keeping the Mess books and generally acting as manager of the Mess. One of the things which I was expected to organise was the Christmas Draw. Naturally I had to put my hand into my own pocket and buy some tickets. So I bought five (this was about average for an impecunious flight lieutenant). I was going to be away for the night of the draw and so I asked someone to let me know if I won anything. I then went home to Guildford and on the morning after the draw, the phone rang. It was my friend at Stradishall.

'What do you want us to do with your turkey?' was the first question.

'Did I really win a turkey?' I replied.

'Yes you did,' he answered.

'If anyone is coming this way, get them to bring it down and I'll meet them and collect it,' I told him. 'Otherwise stick it in the refrigerator until I get back after Christmas.'

'OK,' he replied. 'And shall we do the same with your chicken?'

'Did I win one of those too?'

'Yes!' he said.

'That had better go in the refrigerator as well,' I agreed. 'Did I win anything else?'

'Yes, you won a bottle of brandy and a box of chocolates,' was the answer. 'We have put them in your room.'

'Good,' I said, 'and what did I win with my fifth ticket?'

'Nothing,' he replied.

I immediately declared that the draw *must* have been a fiddle if one of my five tickets didn't win anything. But he didn't seem impressed.

When I got back I arranged for all the members of the staff living in the Mess to have a special dinner one evening: turkey, chicken, brandy and chocolates. The other guys clubbed together and bought several bottles of wine and we had a very excellent staff dinner.

Shortly after this, I think it was about Easter, three other pilots and I were invited to spend a couple of days on HMS *Ark Royal*. By mutual agreement we travelled in my car to the south coast whence we were flown to the carrier 'somewhere in the Channel'. We were duly shown around and overall the visit was a highly instructive two days. Eventually the time came for us to return and again, we were put into a helicopter and flown back to RNAS Ford in Sussex where we had parked the car. We transferred our kit and set off home. The route took us via Winchester, round Guildford and headed for the north orbital route. As we were approaching the Ascot area, I happened to comment to the other three guys that the last time I drove along that road I met a stagecoach pulled by six zebras and I added for good measure: 'This time we will probably meet a herd of elephants.'

The others seemed to think that I was being rather silly, childish even, so they didn't say a lot. We went round the next corner, about a mile from where I had spoken, and there coming down the road were six elephants of various sizes. The silence in the car was so brittle that it would have shattered into a million pieces if anyone had opened their mouth. I was not sure if they thought I had second sight or what, but they paid a lot more attention to me after that. It was several days before I finally admitted that I had known that we were approaching Bertram Mills' winter quarters. But I wonder why I picked on elephants for my forecast?

After Stradishall, I was sent to Central Flying School to learn how to instruct and while I was there, I had a long discussion on spinning with a friend of mine. In particular we were discussing the characteristics of extended spins. We disagreed on a number of points but we did agree that the next time we flew together on a general handling flight, if the weather was good, we would do some extended spinning and see whose theory was correct. Some days later we were detailed for a general handling exercise and the weather was excellent. We boarded our Piston Provost and set off. Climbing to 10,000 feet we carried out the pre-spin checks and we did a couple of 'normal' spins with full patter – we were, after all, potential flying instructors and we were supposed to practise the patter for all the exercises. We then decided on an extended spin. Entry was exactly as normal and we both noted things like rate of roll, rate of yaw, oscillations in pitch, the stability of the spin, the rates of rotation etc., etc. After something in excess of 14 turns, we had both lost count of how many we had completed so we decided to 'recover'. Standard Spin Recovery had its usual effect and the aircraft recovered perfectly normally. The problem was that our own semi-circular canals did not recover. They continued to spin rapidly. So there we were, sitting in an aircraft which was trimmed for straight and level flight and which was actually flying straight and level, because we had had the sense to let go of the controls, and yet both of us were convinced that the aircraft was spinning rapidly in the opposite direction to the original spin. Our eyes could see that this was not happening but the rest of our bodies were convinced that it was. Having thought about this disorientation problem before we started we both managed to let well alone but it was an eerie feeling to 'know that you are spinning' while your eyes are telling you that you are approximately straight and level. It took a lot of self control to wait patiently while the brain sorted out fact from fiction. I have no doubt that had we been in cloud we would not have been able to leave the aircraft to its own devices and rely on its built-in stability to keep us the right way up. Indeed a lot of people have crashed, trying to correct a situation which didn't exist except in their brains. Spatial disorientation is a killer if allowed to take control.

The next extended spin in which I was involved was after going to Valley to instruct. My student and I were detailed for an exercise of high-level aerobatics. This involved climbing to 35,000 feet where I had to demonstrate a series of aerobatics, showing the student the various tricks needed to complete each manoeuvre at that height. This is an extremely difficult exercise and frequently, several of my demonstrations don't work out exactly as I intended – and about three-quarters of the students' aerobatics don't work out as either of us intended. This is no problem, as one of the reasons for the exercise is to revise the students' ability to recover from 'unusual attitudes'. During one loop with the student flying the aircraft, he slightly over-pitched and the aircraft entered a spin going vertically upwards. As you will appreciate, the remaining speed bled off rapidly and the aircraft paused as it stopped going upwards and forwards and started to tumble downwards. I noticed that the altimeter was reading 43,000 feet. When the 'tumble' had stabilised, I went into my patter and pointed out that the aircraft appeared to be spinning to the right. I took normal recovery action and was surprised to see the direction of spin apparently reverse and the spin continue unabated. I pointed out to the student that this indicated we had been in an inverted spin initially so, once more allowing the spin to stabilise, I again took standard spin recovery and as expected, the aircraft came out of its spin and was put back into a full-power climb. I told my student that at the bottom of the recovery manoeuvre, we were passing 9,000 feet. I have no idea how many turns we completed, but we had managed to lose 34,000 feet doing it. We could have recovered more quickly, but I wanted to include the full patter of my recovery because deliberate inverted spins are not approved and it was probably the only chance we would ever have of seeing one. It took a long time to climb back up to 35,000 to continue the exercise.

Shortly after I had been posted to Valley I decided that this would be a good moment to take up sailing, so, one Saturday morning, I drove into Holyhead and went to look for the sailing club. I asked several people for directions but they all seemed fairly vague. Eventually at the end of the promenade, I spotted some workmen doing some repairs so I asked them if there was a sailing club.

'Oh yes,' was the reply, 'why do you want to know?'

'I was thinking of joining them and learning how to sail properly,' I replied.

'In that case,' he said, 'pick up that shovel.' So I did.

'Right then,' he remarked, 'now you are a member of the Holyhead Sailing Club, you can help us building the slipway. I'm the chairman and these others are the committee.' So I took my coat off and got on with it. When we had finished the slipway – a three-month job – we started on the club house, but if the tide was in and the slipway under water, we all sailed instead. After a while I decided that I really ought to have a boat of my own and so I looked for, and bought, a Firefly. This is a fairly light dinghy, normal crew is two but it can be sailed single handed. The first time I put it on the water, I asked my flight commander who, being a naval officer, ought to know a bit about boats, if he would like to come with me. He was in favour and so the following Saturday afternoon we set off for a local lake where we proceeded to rig the mast, fix the sails and launch into the water. The inevitable happened and within a reasonably short period, one of us did something he shouldn't have done, and the boat capsized. We both surfaced and with an effort righted the boat. There was no way we could board it, full of water, so we decided to swim it ashore. Here we managed to bail it out slowly and we were nearly ready to re-launch when my crew's wife arrived and fell about laughing. She talked good sense into the two soaked idiots standing on the edge of the lake and she then set off for their home, some three miles down the road. We, the soaked idiots, unrigged the boat and then got into the car and followed her. By the time we arrived there were two dressing gowns hung on the kitchen door and a note saying 'Don't you dare!' So we stripped off all our wet clothes, put on the dressing gowns and went upstairs to find the bath full of hot water. It was a giant Victorian bath so we both got in and within a couple of minutes my flight commander's wife had arrived with tea. She poured out the drink and passed us food, while we wallowed in the hot water and gradually thawed out. Then we got dressed into dry clothes and we all went to the local pub for some anti-freeze, before returning to the lake to collect the boat. All in all it was a pretty unsuccessful sail but a very pleasant day for all that. At least it was until my flight commander's wife pointed out that her husband used to be in submarines and was only really happy when he was underwater. Trust me to pick one of those!

While I am talking about sailing boats, one of the problems facing all dinghy sailors is finding a crew. The owner of a boat normally steers and looks after the mainsail, but he needs somebody to control the jib and the centreboard and to lean out at impossible angles, to stop the boat from heeling over too far and to ensure that it is going as fast as possible. Being a relative newcomer to the art of sailing, I always managed to get the leftovers, because naturally the better crews were always snapped up by the better helmsmen. One Saturday afternoon I was starting to get a bit desperate when I noticed a slim, dark-haired, long-legged girl hanging around, and since beggars can't be choosers. I asked her if she would like to crew for me. To my surprise she said yes. We did nothing spectacular in the race, but at least we finished without capsizing. She agreed to crew for me on several occasions after that and, finally, after a lot of persuasion became my permanent crew. But I had to marry her first. That was quite a party. Our wedding was in Holyhead on the morning of the Officers' Mess Christmas party. So all the guests simply transferred from one party to the next one. My best man and the 'head' bridesmaid started their party at 11.30 am and finished it at breakfast time the next day. They deserved to enjoy themselves.

One of the favourite sports in Wales is to switch to speaking Welsh as soon as an obvious visitor comes into the room, and then talk about him without the visitor knowing what is being said. During my early days in Anglesey I learnt a few Welsh expressions which I thought might come in useful. One weekend I had been home to Guildford and I was returning to Anglesey on the Sunday evening and I decided to stop at a small inn in Betws-y-Coed for a drink and a bite to eat. There were four locals in the bar chatting away in Welsh and when I had ordered my drink and a sandwich they persuaded the youngest of the four to go to the bar and get some more drinks and at the same time say something rude in Welsh to the 'foreigner'. So he went to the bar, ordered his drinks (in Welsh) looked across at me and smiled and made a rather rude comment – again in Welsh. Not to be outdone, I smiled and replied with something much ruder – also in Welsh. His associates burst out laughing, he went rather red in the face and they all switched to English and joined me for a chat. I suppose it was a bit unsporting for a Englishman to learn to speak some rude words in Welsh.

One of the most terrifying things that can happen to a pilot is to find that his aircraft is on fire. I'm glad to say that on only three occasions have I come across this phenomenon and only one of those concerned an aircraft I was in. The first two times concerned aircraft landing ... But let me tell you about them. They all three occurred when I was based at Valley in Anglesey. We always had a duty instructor in the Tower and one day it was my turn. I sat there, probably only half awake, but with one ear cocked to the radio. I didn't know why at the time but I suddenly told the local controller to overshoot the aircraft on finals and hold everyone. Sure enough, the aircraft on finals went around and the controller looked at me as I reached over his arm and hit the big red crash bell. It was only about then that my brain caught up with my mouth and hands. As I turned round, I watched an Aer Lingus Dakota cross the hedge of the out-of-wind runway, with his port engine well and truly on fire. I had heard his 'Mayday' in the background – the volume was turned well down in the tower on 121.5 mhz. The crash crew were on the job in no time flat and the fire was extinguished and the passengers evacuated in record time. The passengers were taken into the terminal building and offered 'refreshment' and the airfield resumed its normal operations. Later that day, another aircraft arrived from Dublin with a replacement engine and some engineers. The passengers were transferred to that aircraft and completed their journey while the slightly sooty aircraft was flown out the following morning with the replacement engine in place.

The second fire I observed was also when I was at Valley. I was not the duty instructor. It is just as well probably, because the guy who was on watch did a superb job and probably saved the aircraft and its pilot. A student joined the circuit in his single-seat Vampire and as he came in to land he announced that he did not have the necessary three green undercarriage lights and was going around. As the aircraft passed the Tower, it was noticed that his aircraft was on fire. The single-seat aircraft are not fitted with an ejection seat, so the duty instructor grabbed the microphone from the controller and put it to 'transmit'. He then 'pattered' the whole of a very tight, low-level circuit leading to a wheels up, flapless approach. As the student and his aircraft came up to the airfield boundary, the patter went something like this: 'Speed should be 95 knots, it doesn't matter if you are one or two knots fast, that's very nice, hold it there just off the ground, let it settle onto the runway, OK pull the high pressure cock off [this stops the engine], keep the wings level, very nice – keep the wings level, you are nearly stopped, now undo your harness and parachute straps, just stopping, *now get out and run – you are on fire!*' The student got out and ran. And was totally uninjured. He hadn't know about the fire (the fire warning light is just to the right of the gunsight and not very 'attention getting'). The duty instructor, decided – quite rightly I think – that if any one of the other four or five aircraft in the circuit saw the fire they would have blurted out some remark or other on the radio, which would have caused the student with the fire not only to panic but probably to muck up the landing as well. With the Air Traffic radio transmitting, no one else could get a word in. I would like to think that I would have been equally quick witted, but I fear that it's wishful thinking.

My third fire was much more personal. I had been on a dual low-level navigation trip round the Cheshire plain. Having completed the route, I told the student to climb to an appropriate flight level above 10,000 feet, and to head back towards Valley. There was a layer of cloud between 1,500 feet and 4,000 feet but visibility above was excellent. As we passed 11,000 feet I was alerted by a very bright red light in the centre top of the instrument panel. Naturally, my brain went into neutral instantly but when it had recovered, I reached past the student to turn off the low pressure fuel cock, and to flick the radio change over switch to No. 2 box, which was always pre-set on 243 mhz transmit. I transmitted a 'Mayday' call and, as the speed fell, pressed the fire extinguisher. In the Vampire, the fire detection switches are not resetting so I had no way of knowing if the fire was out except by flying a tight turn and looking back to see if I had a trail of smoke. As far as I could see, we didn't. The D + D Cell at Preston Centre gave us a heading and distance to go to Shawbury. I remember thinking that 34 miles was a hell of a long way to try to glide from 11,000 feet into wind. They told me that there was nowhere nearer, although they did mention a disused airfield at Slaep, but we were in cloud when we passed it. It became obvious that we were not going to get to Shawbury so I had all the time in the world to brief my student and to remind him about how to 'fly' a parachute. At about 2,000 feet we jettisoned the canopy and at 1,500 I ordered him to bail out. I carried on a bit further and at some 500 feet above ground level, I followed him. All the equipment worked perfectly but when I looked down I found myself descending towards some 33,000 volt power lines. I pulled on the rear lift webs to drift back, away from the cables and hit the ground an almighty wallop but I missed the power lines and the farmhouse which had materialised from behind me. There was a nasty crunching noise as I hit the ground so I let myself fall down the pile of brick rubble which I had managed to land on and I slid myself on to a patch of reasonably clean grass. Next problem was to attract attention. There was smoke coming out of the farmhouse chimney so I got my whistle out and blew loud and long. After a few minutes a lovely lady looked over the wall. She was at least 50 years old and still had her hair in curlers and her bedroom slippers on. 'What's all that noise?' she asked.

I apologised for disturbing her, told her that my aircraft had crashed somewhere 'over there' and asked if she was on the telephone. She was, so I asked her to pop back indoors and dial 999 and tell the police that my aircraft had crashed, that I was there and that I needed an ambulance. She was back in a very few minutes with her hair curlers out, but still in her slippers and, being typically British, she had a tray with a pot of tea, a milk jug, a bowl of sugar and what looked like the best china. It was strong, but one of the best drinks I have ever had. While I was sipping it, my student walked up – he was totally uninjured – and then two of the farm workers arrived out of breath. They had seen it all happen and had run over to see if they could help. Some 15–20 minutes after the accident, the RAF ambulance arrived, picked me up and took me to Shawbury where we were given lunch and afterwards flown back to Valley in an elderly Avro Anson. That evening, as I lay in the Station Medical Centre, with a compression fracture of the spine and seven broken bones in my left foot, there was a knock on the door and in came my student and his very pregnant wife. Not only that, but they were carrying a case of Guinness. Since his wife was pregnant she couldn't drink, and since he was detailed for night flying later that night, he couldn't drink either, so I had to drink it all. It can be hard work being a flying instructor.

While I was at Valley I was given a very good lesson on human behaviour. I was sent for by the Station Commander, Group Captain Rivett-Carnack (I think that's the correct spelling but if not I apologise).

'I want you to go up to the Airmen's Mess and carry out a surprise stock check of all the food. When you have done it, report back here to me personally.' 'Yes, sir,' I replied and headed for the Mess.

I went into the Warrant Officers' office and informed him that I had been ordered to carry out a complete stock check: 'Call I have the stock books please.' He handed them to me and explained that he was just entering that day's issues, so I sat down and entered them from the ration chits on his desk. We then went into the storerooms and started counting and weighing. With a population of some 2,000 people on the camp, it was a long and tedious job but eventually we got to the end. The time was now 17.45 hours, work on the station had stopped three-quarters of an hour ago and, by the sound of it, everyone had gone home. I debated whether to go back to Station Headquarters and see if the Station Commander was still there. I decided I would, fortunately, because I found him still sitting in his office waiting for me. In I went.

'Everything was fine, sir,' I reported, 'except for the sugar which was about seven pounds short, the tea which was about four pounds over and the butter which was about two pounds short.'

'Good,' he replied. 'If you had told me that they were all correct. I would have sent you back to do a proper check. Tea, sugar and butter are all bound to be slightly out. If they are not, there is a fiddle going on.' He then offered me a lift to the Officers' Mess on his way home.

Another occasion when I was the duty instructor sticks in my memory. It was a nice autumn day and the wind at RAF Valley was light westerly. There were no clouds in the sky and the visibility was about ten miles. At about three o'clock in the afternoon the outside air temperature was dropping steadily and I had just been given my nth cup of tea. I noticed that the wind was slowly backing through south and looking to my right, in the direction of Holyhead, I saw that the top of Holyhead hill had been covered by a small cap of mist. I thought about that for all of 15 seconds and then turned to the controllers. I told the local controller to cancel all take-off traffic and then I told the approach controller to put out an immediate recall of all aircraft. Pilots were to be instructed to return as quickly as possible. The controllers looked at me rather strangely but did what they had been told to do. The aircraft moving on the ground all had to return to their squadron dispersal and a few minutes later the phone started to ring.

'Why have you cancelled all take offs?' seemed to be the general theme but not put quite so politely.

'The weather is clamping,' was my reply. This stimulated some rather harsh remarks but I ignored them. About five minutes later, OC Flying came up to the Tower. 'What's going on Rufus?' he asked.

'The weather is clamping and I have issued an immediate recall and stopped all take offs, sir,' I replied.

'I see,' he said and not one more word did he speak. He just stood there like a silent nemesis.

After about ten more minutes, the approach controller told me that the last aircraft was just entering the circuit. We all watched it land and taxi back to its squadron. Silence reigned and I slowly got more and more depressed.

About three minutes after the last aircraft had landed – but it felt like three hours to me – the entire airfield suddenly went into fog over a period of about 25 seconds. The wing commander's mouth opened and it had much the same effect on the controllers. OC Flying turned to me: 'I don't know how you did it, Rufus, but thank you. We might well have lost some of the aircraft if you hadn't recalled them. I must admit I thought you had been having a brainstorm or something. Let's go and open the Officers' Mess bar. The drinks are on me!' So we did and they were.

All good things come to an end and at the scheduled time I was posted. For once I was posted to an administrative job. I can't complain, I had been on flying posts continuously since 1943 and it was an interesting job. I was destined to become the Station Adjutant at RAF Wildenrath. This was by far the largest Air Force base in Germany and I looked forward to the challenge.

5

After Valley: 1958–72

Wildenrath

Arriving in Germany, via the military train from Ostende I soon settled into the routine. The station commander was very helpful, he realised that this was all new to me, so he gave me 48 hours to get the job sorted out. I had to put in a bit of overtime at first but it was not long before I got my act in order.

Quite early on I realised that motoring accidents and offences were going to play a big part in my work so I invented the post of Station Road Safety Officer and appointed myself as the first one. This enabled me to build a road safety organisation throughout the station so that we could concentrate our attention on preventing accidents and also on training everyone else to drive in accordance with the German law rather that the much more woolly British law. I was draconian in my treatment of motoring offenders and I used to take licences from drivers for quite trivial offences. For a first offence, the driver lost his licence for a month, for the second he lost it for six months and for a third offence, he lost it for the remainder of his tour in Germany. In every case, it was instant justice and the offender had to leave his car at the side of the road and walk from then on.

He then had to find someone with a licence to drive it home for him. I know it all sounds pretty brutal, but it worked. There were very few second offenders and no third-time losers. Naturally, the 'offence' had to be something black or white such as failing to 'halt!' at a halt sign rather than an offence which was possibly defensible such as driving without due care and attention. We were the only RAF Station in Germany whose accident rate did not increase over the next two years. That's not to say that we didn't have any accidents but we managed to hold the figures level. I employed all sorts of gimmicks to get the drivers aware of what they were doing. I had specialised police lecturers come and explain the German traffic law. I obtained English language copies of the German 'highway code'; I put out intercepts to pick up drinking drivers. I impounded unroadworthy vehicles and on the whole I was a right little Hitler. But we did have the best accident record in Germany. I hope and think that this, in part, resulted from my campaign.

As Station Adjutant, I didn't get many chances to get airborne but I managed a few flights. As I was the only Vampire QFI on the Station, I was invited to check people out, before they flew our one and only Vampire aircraft. I rather blotted my copybook one day. The Air Officer Commanding decided that he would get checked out in the Vampire, so I was sent for. We had a normal full briefing and got airborne. There were no handling problems with his upper air work and after a couple of circuits and bumps he had the landing attitude and height pretty well sorted out. At the end of the flight we walked back to the squadron offices and I de-briefed him on the way. Arriving at the squadron commander's office, we went in and the CO turned to me and said, 'Fit solo then, Rufus?'

'No, sir,' I replied.

'What do you mean?' he asked.

'Like any experienced pilot,' I told him. 'He can fly the aircraft OK but he doesn't know any of the emergency drills.

Until he does, he should always have another pilot with him.'

The AOC turned to me and said: 'You're absolutely correct old boy.' And walked out. The squadron commander never again invited me to check anyone out in the Vampire.

After I had been at Wildenrath for about eight months, we held an Air Day, for the benefit of the local population. Two of the items which we put on have stuck in my memory. The display was declared formally open and some ten seconds later one of our Photographic Reconnaissance Canberras flew down the line of the crowd dropping a series of photo-flash pyrotechnics. It pulled up, turned into the traffic pattern, dropped its wheels and landed. A motorcycle drove over to it and removed the camera magazine and rushed it to the caravan in the middle of the airfield where we had placed the mobile field photographic unit. In a very short space of time, more motorcycle dispatch riders had driven away from the caravan towards the crowd, where they distributed glossy prints of that section of the crowd, which had been taken just a few minutes earlier. The crowd were told to give them a good rinse when they got home as there had been no time to rinse them properly before issuing them. The spectators were most impressed, because they could see themselves in the photographs. The next item which has remained in my memory all these years was the Pembroke display. The Pembroke is a small, high-wing, twin-engine aircraft which normally carries up to eight passengers. The display aircraft took off after a very short run and climbed away steeply. It flew past low and pretty fast for a Pembroke, pulled up and feathered one engine. It then flew past in the opposite direction, pulling up again and feathering the second engine. This time it flew past more slowly and as soon as it was past, it restarted first one then the other engine, completed a tight circuit and landed. Turning off at the end of the runway, the aircraft taxied slowly back to the crowd and halted. The door opened and

26 fully equipped members of the RAF Regiment got out and marched away. The crowd were thunderstruck. So was I! What I didn't find out until later was that our second Pembroke with all the guys on board had been waiting at the end of the runway where a clump of trees hides the taxi way. When the very light 'aerobatic' Pembroke landed and taxied back it was swapped for the other aircraft which had the same registration letters painted on the side. It made a wonderful leg pull.

One of the more interesting of my duties while at Wildenrath was my post of Station Security Officer. This enabled me to find out a number of things of which I had 'a need to know'. On one such occasion I was informed that one of the locally enlisted security guards was being paid a considerable sum of money each month by the East German Embassy. When I had a spare moment, I phoned my police warrant officer and asked him where this man was on duty. When asked why, I told him about the guy's private source of income. The warrant officer's reaction was immediate. 'I'll have him off the station within the hour, sir.'

'You won't,' I replied. 'You will never sack that man. What you will do is ensure that he is only used on non-sensitive tasks. We know who he is. If you sack him they will simply suborn another guy and we won't know who that one is.' He took my point. (This was all nearly 40 years ago so the story can be told now.)

Having always been keen on Survival, and Escape and Evasion exercises I was delighted to be co-opted by the station commander to make up the numbers on a couple of exercises. The first one was a locally organised E & E exercise lasting 48 hours and the second was the full Winter Survival Course in Bavaria. The short exercise was fun because it was a summer exercise intended to keep crews fit and to polish up their map-reading skills as well as practising their evasion techniques. The CO and I made up a 'crew' and it's not true to say that I carried all his kit. He helped, while I was cooking his meals. We had to go to a series of map references without being 'caught' by the defending force and we were scheduled to arrive at an RAF unit 'Somewhere in Germany' at 06.00 hrs. We actually arrived just after midnight and so we lit a fire and fried potatoes which we had 'gleaned' on our way. We lit the fire in the centre of the road as we didn't want to set fire to the forest. As the other 'evaders' arrived they joined us and the fire got bigger and bigger. I suspect that the tarmac would have needed patching by dawn.

The other exercise took a fortnight and was located in Bavaria. There were lectures early and late each day but in the middle of the day – sort of from 09.30 to 16.30 – we went out on the hills and practised our skiing. The RAF provided the equipment and some highly skilled instructors and we provided the effort. It also helped to get us fit for the second week. During week two, in the wee small hours of Monday morning, we were dropped off with a small load of equipment which had to provide shelter and sustenance for the remainder of the week. We had to find out where we were, and then travel to an RV where we were required to build shelters and 'survive'. There were a number of survival-orientated tasks which we had to perform and we also had to scatter from the 'camp area' when it was attacked. The 'enemy' consisted of German Army NCOs from one of their training camps nearby. They were disgustingly fit and could outrun us with no trouble. So we had to be crafty. The course was split into six 'teams' of four. In the event, our team were the only ones who were not caught at any time during the whole week. Those who were caught, were taken back several miles and allowed to 'escape'. We were not caught because, after they had made the initial mistake of electing me as team leader, I insisted on travelling off the tracks and three-quarters of the way up each mountain instead of in the valleys. Our 'prize' for being the top group was, that at the end of the week, we were the first team

released by the umpires and by travelling fast, we managed
to get back to the hotel in which we were billeted, first. The
hotel had a total of four baths for guests. Believe you me,
after a week in the Bavarian hills in midwinter, a long soak in
a hot bath was a really wonderful prize, and we enjoyed it
even more when we found that the hot water had run out for
the late-comers. The station commander decided to take his
wife and car with him and had suggested that my wife Olive
and I accompanied them on the drive down to Bavaria. We
put the girls into the Hotel's modern annexe while we were
in the less comfortable main building. When the course was
over, the station commander and I waited behind and spent
the weekend 'relaxing'. I managed to organise some skiing
instruction for Olive from one of the school instructors.

Many a time during my two and a half years in Germany,
people would come to me with good reasons why they
should be sent on compassionate leave. As Station Adjutant,
it became my job to find the quickest way of getting them
back to the UK. There was usually some form of transportation which I could lean on to help these guys get home
a.s.a.p. but I think my record was on the occasion when one
particular airman came to see me, who had an excellent
reason for getting home quickly. I sent him to his barrack
block to change, collect his kit and come back to see me.
While he was doing this I got on the phone and found that an
aircraft had just called on the radio to taxi out prior to its take
off to return to the UK. A quick relay to the captain and he
agreed to hold his aircraft on the ground for me. As soon as
the airman arrived, he was bundled into a car and driven to
the beginning of the runway where this aircraft was sitting
with its engines running. The airman was put aboard and
within 45 minutes of his coming to see me, he was on the
ground in England. Here I had arranged for him to be met
and taken to the local railway station to catch a train home. It
is extraordinary what you can set up with a bit of imagination and effort but it all paid off in the long run when the

airmen on the station started to appreciate that the RAF was all one large family.

Sometimes, it worked the other way round. One of the advantages of a posting to Germany was that we could buy a car totally tax free. This represented a huge saving and so just about everybody out there took advantage of the concession. We could import a car into the UK on change of residence, if it had been 'in our use and possession for 365 days'. Needless to say people would come to me and say that they had not completed their year for some reason or other and could they extend their tour. Naturally I did my best to help them provided there were no overriding Service reasons why they should go back to the UK on their tour-expiry date. Many a guy ended up doing a couple of months extra in Germany so that he could import his 'duty free' car into the UK without having to pay tax on it.

One of the more interesting tasks which I set myself at Wildenrath was organising an annual motor show. As I have said, one of the chief attractions of a posting to Germany was the fact that we could buy a motor car free of all tax, but it was not always possible to determine which was the best value for money. As I consequence, I decided to organise a motor show to be held on a Saturday in August. I wrote to all the local car dealers inviting them to attend and to bring all their demonstrators. I advertised the show everywhere I could think of. Admission was free and the dealers were not charged for attending. The Wildenrath Motor Club was only too pleased to help with the organisation. There were many acres of concrete on the airfield and I was given permission to use them for the show. I managed, eventually, to get just about every make and model of car that was available at that time and I had obviously done something right because the day dawned bright, sunny and warm. At about eight-thirty in the morning, I got a phone call in my quarters. It was the main gate.

'Sir,' the airman said, 'there's a German here who says he has brought your cars.'

'Yes, that's right,' I replied. 'Ask him to drive down to the Air Movements apron and I'll meet him there.'

'Are they really your cars, sir?' he asked.

'Yes that's right, they are for me,' I replied.

'Gosh, I wish I was an officer,' was his next remark.

When I got there I understood what he meant. There was a transporter fully loaded with: a Lancia Flamina GT, an Alfa Romeo 2 litre Spyder, a Facel Vega Excellence, and a Ferrari 250 GTO. I was rather impressed myself. The other vehicles at the show were all driven there under their own steam and by half past nine there were about 90 cars ready for inspection. The advertising had said 'gates open at 11 o'clock' and we in fact opened up half an hour early to prevent congestion. All told it was estimated that 20,000 people came to the show. The salesmen were put on their mettle because at three o'clock I announced that potential buyers could road test the cars on the airfield. Many people had a shortlist of cars which they considered buying and this gave them a chance to compare them on the same 'road' one after the other. As expected the salesmen were all trying to outdo each other and when the driving got a bit too wild, I called a 15-minute truce. They all simmered down a bit then as they realised I wouldn't allow dangerous driving. The guy who had sent the transporter which had arrived first, came bustling over as soon as I announced test drives. 'Herr Heald,' he said, 'I am a bit worried. If anyone wants to buy one of my very expensive cars, of course he can have a test drive but I would not want to think that they might get damaged.'

'I quite understand,' I replied. 'I think the answer is that they are uninsured, which is why they came on a transporter. Isn't that right?' He got the message.

'But perhaps if you and your lady would like to have a drive in the Ferrari?' Once we got all 24 spark plugs firing, that car went very well, to say the least.

A few days later I spoke to the guy who was the Peugeot, Simca, Standard, and Rover dealer. 'How did you get on last Saturday?' I asked him.

'Pretty well thank you, Herr Heald,' he replied, 'I think we sold 60 cars that we would not otherwise have sold.' I knew that a lot of people had been waiting for a motor show before committing themselves but an extra 60 cars represented a lot of money – and that was only one dealer.

I think I had the worst week of my life when I was at Wildenrath. A friend of mine went over to the UK to complete a flight safety course and his wife Nancy, who was about six months pregnant, came to stay with us in our quarters in a German village called Am Zoppenberg a few miles from the airfield. On Monday afternoon, at five minutes to five, I was told that one of our aircraft had crashed, killing both the crew. I then had to try and organise a crash guard for the wreckage and I had to get all the essential back-up of tents, and rations and that sort of thing sorted out and transported to the crash scene. It was late when I finished and it was only when I got home that I realised that the navigator in the crashed aircraft had been my friend's navigator. He was just flying with the crash pilot to keep in practice. As you will understand, Nancy was more than a little upset. Next morning I had to organise the board of inquiry to investigate the accident and I also had to detail people off and brief them to form what is called the Committee of Adjustment. This looks after all the personal details on behalf of the next of kin. Then I had to arrange the funerals of the crew and I had to get their next of kin over from England. The navigator's parents were elderly and they decided that they would rather travel by boat. So I booked a passage for them and the squadron arranged for one of the other pilots to drive to Ostende in his car to pick them up. He collected them OK but on the way back, in Belgium, the car was involved in a head on collision with a

German fuel tanker. The car driver was in hospital with a broken leg and other injuries but the parents were both very seriously injured and, sadly, they both died in hospital that day. Now I had to organise the transportation of the bodies from Belgium, through Holland and into Germany. Then I had to get clearance for them to be buried in the military section of the cemetery, next to their son, and I had to get their next of kin over for the funeral. By Friday morning I thought that I had managed to get everything under control until, just before lunchtime, when an airman on a motor-cycle went under the wheels of a large lorry. So I had yet another set of arrangements to make. Finally, at five-thirty I set off for home. It had been a bad week and I was dog tired. On arrival I found the girls sitting in floods of tears. Eventually I got them to tell me the problem. They had been told that my friend Bob, Nancy's husband, had been killed on his way back from the UK in an aircraft from Marham which was coming over to Wildenrath. They had been told that he was coming back early and this was the only aircraft due in that day. I tried hard to tell them that they were talking rubbish and by about eight o'clock they had simmered down a bit. At half past eight, Bob arrived in person to prove that he had not been in the crashed bomber. He had hitched a lift in another aircraft to Cologne and got another lift out from there. The girls cheered up then. I was more than a bit shattered by my week's work so I went to bed early.

However at about eleven-thirty, there was a banging on the wall of my bedroom and Bob put his head round the door. 'Nan is having a miscarriage – where is the nearest doctor?' I briefed him on the whereabouts of an army doctor who happened to live a few doors down the street. Olive got up and went to help Nan and I went and got the house switched on, the doors unlocked and I also got my car out and warmed it up. The doctor arrived, went to see Nan and a few minutes later came out. 'She must go to hospital at once,' he said. 'I'll phone for an ambulance.' 'No need,' I replied, 'my car makes down into a bed, we can take her in that.' Bob rushed in and a few moments later reappeared with Nan in his arms. She was placed on the fully reclining seat, Bob got in the back and I set off. We completed the seven miles of mainly built up area in six minutes. Thank goodness I had a two-tone horn. We delivered Nan to the hospital and they told us to go home and come back in the morning. I drove a lot slower on the way back. It had definitely not been a good week and I did not want to cap it by collecting a ticket for speeding. To finish the story off, all went well, Nan and Bob had a super child who went on to row for the winning crew in at least two university boat races, so it couldn't have done him any lasting harm.

When I had completed my two-and-a-half year stint in Germany, I was posted back to the UK and following the inevitable period of leave, I went to the School of Refresher Flying at RAF Strubby, in Lincolnshire. This was part of the RAF College of Air Warfare and our parent unit was at RAF Manby. After a short stay in a farmhouse at Maltby-le-Marsh, I look over one of the married quarters in the town of Alford. Having completed the flying refresher course, which happened to be on my old friends the Meteor aircraft, I stayed on as a member of the staff. We used to get a number of senior officers going through the school, after they had been flying a desk in the Ministry of Defence or at Command Headquarters.

On one occasion I had a fairly senior Group Captain as my student and we were airborne in a Meteor VII. We were scheduled to examine the critical speed handling of the aircraft on one engine and to determine the Group Captain's personal critical speed. Without being too technical, the critical speed is the minimum speed at which a particular pilot can maintain control of a particular aircraft with one engine failed under the worst conditions. This means shutting down one engine and flying at maximum power on the other engine with wheels and flaps extended to give maximum drag and then gradually reducing speed until the pilot starts to lose control. He then recovers back into fully controlled flight. The exercise has to be done at low level (1,500 feet) in order to get maximum power. Initially I demonstrated that the aircraft critical speed was 130 knots and having made sure that my student knew exactly what to do I gave him control in order to determine what the critical speed was, with him flying the aircraft. In many cases, the minimum speed in a Meteor, which has mechanically operated controls, is dependent on pilot strength. He started off correctly at about 150 knots at full power on one engine and with the other one shut down. Lifting the nose to reduce speed he gradually applied more and more rudder to counteract the turning effect of the live engine. At 135 knots, the rudder cable parted: I know that the aircraft completed two flick rolls, before I managed to get the second engine wound up, and the first one throttled back, and I was able to get the aircraft under control again, but we were very, very near the ground. All four rudder pedals had gone fully forward and we had no rudder control at all. When my pulse rate had dropped to under 300, I very slowly and carefully returned to base, landed, and taxied to the dispersal where we parked. We got out in total silence, completed the technical log, went into the crew room, changed out of our flying kit, got into my car and went back to the Mess where we both proceeded to consume large quantities of alcohol. Or in simple terms, we got very drunk. Nothing was going to get either of us into an aircraft again that day. The critical speed exercise is probably the most dangerous flight there is in a twin-engine aircraft. You deliberately go right to the edge of controllability, near the ground. And if it does go all pear shaped, then, although we wear parachutes, there is not the slightest chance of getting out before hitting the ground. We were astonishingly lucky that the aircraft just happened to stop its uncontrolled roll, roughly the right way up, and we able to fly it home, otherwise it would have certainly killed both of us.

I got some experience of professional aircraft photography one day, when I was tasked to fly a BBC cameraman who wanted to take photographs of Vulcan bombers carrying out in-flight refuelling from a Victor Tanker aircraft. On that occasion the radar unit with whom I was working thought I was a Vulcan as I was using a Waddington Callsign – Waddington being the Vulcan Bomber base. In fact we were flying in a Meteor T VII. A two-seat aircraft with a maximum endurance of about one hour and no navigation aids as opposed to a four-engine, long-range bomber with 'several' hours' endurance. They managed to just about run me out of fuel. Indeed I had cause to ask the cameraman if he had any film left.

'Yes, a little,' was the reply.

'Good, keep your camera handy. You have a good chance of getting some very dramatic pictures which should make the 9 o'clock news,' I told him.

'Oh! What?' he asked.

'Us!' was the answer. 'I'm afraid they have run us out of fuel and it doesn't look as though we are going to make it. At least you should be able to make a packet from the photographs of our crash.'

He seemed to think that I was joking at first but went all silent when I persuaded him that I was not. I think he was secretly a bit disappointed when we got on to the ground safely without a crash, following a flame-out pattern from 20,000 feet having glided the last 50 miles. The cloud base was very low and we were lucky that I was able to keep the aircraft positioned in a spiral overhead. When they looked in the tanks, there was no fuel visible anywhere. The radar controller got a flea in his ear when I got to a phone. He just hadn't appreciated that our aircraft had only short endurance and no navigational equipment at all and we were totally dependent on the radar unit for keeping us within range of an airfield. I suppose in some ways it was my fault for not telling him that although I was using a Waddington callsign, I was not a Vulcan bomber with several hours' endurance but a two-seat training aircraft with an absolute maximum of about one-hour endurance.

One day at Strubby I was walking towards the hangar with the Wing Commander when we stopped and listened. Somebody was having one hell of a ticking off for something. The language got pretty strong, even for those days, and the poor miscreant's antecedents were traced back a very long way ending with the words, 'I should have had more sense than to put a stupid black Negro on a job that required brains.' The Wing Commander and I looked at each other, horrified by the remark we had heard. Out of the hangar came a very red-faced airman of West Indian descent, looking highly embarrassed, followed by a very angry corporal who obviously came from West Africa since he was a lot blacker than the airman he had been ticking off. Somehow both the Wing Commander and I decided that any comment on racial abuse, or what is nowadays referred to as 'political correctness', would be superfluous.

While on the subject of senior officers, there was another interesting flight I made one day. My 'student' was my own Commander-in-Chief who was converting on to the Meteor. We had been carrying out some circuits and landings and everything had been going OK. On one particular circuit, we were on base leg, coming up to our final turn, when an aircraft which was carrying out an instrument approach called. It was evident that we were going to conflict with him, so I instructed my 'student' to overshoot. He acknowledged this and tightened his turn to about 75 degrees of bank – to keep inside the instrument aircraft. He then selected undercarriage up, and flap up. The trouble was that he had not increased power and we dropped like the proverbial brick. There was a gulp from me and I came on the controls. Both throttles were moved fully forward – never mind the temperatures which went well over the limits – I rolled the wings level and tried very hard not to hit the ground. We actually got down into ground cushion effect before I managed to halt the descent and the aircraft slowly accelerated as the engines wound up to their maximum of 14,700 RPM. Having got the aircraft back into a climb and cleared the trees and things, I handed control back to my Commander-in-Chief; but not before I had told him what I thought of pilots who did that sort of thing. I was using some very basic English and he went bright red up the back of his neck. For the rest of the flight, relations were somewhat strained, to say the least. After another two or three circuits, we landed, taxied in, parked and got out.

The flight sergeant came hurrying over, 'Everything OK with the aircraft, sir?' he asked the C-in-C.

'Don't ask me, ask the captain,' was the answer.

I reassured the flight sergeant that there were no problems and the C-in-C turned to me. 'I have never been spoken to like that in all my life! I won't forget what you said to me Rufus!'

'Oh, that's OK, sir,' I replied. 'As far as I'm concerned you have had your rollicking and the incident is closed.'

'Well it's not ruddy well closed as far as I'm concerned,' he announced, and walked off back to the VIP office. He was quite right, he didn't forget. That year he sent for my Annual Confidential Report and added a personal recommendation for promotion.

Altogether I spent just under three years at Strubby before I was posted to the Ministry of Defence. Here I was working in the Directorate of Flight Safety and my personal task was to write the whole of the Flight Safety section of the RAF Magazine, *Air Clues*. This is a monthly magazine and the centre 10 pages were all the result of my writings and were focused on Flight Safety. It was a fascinating job because every accident and incident in the whole of the Air Force ended up on my desk and I would analyse them carefully until I had a bundle from each of which I considered that a lesson could be learnt. I wrote under the name of *Wing Commander S H P Spry, DSO DFC AFC*, and as such I had to know all about every aircraft in the Air Force, and quite a lot of others. Fortunately I could discuss the cases with the rest of the Directorate's staff or I could contact the station concerned or the manufacturer of the aircraft. The centre-page spread was always given over to some academic subject or other, so every month I had to write three to four thousand words for that alone. Trying to find interesting subjects after the first six months was a task on its own. One of the more fascinating concerned metal fatigue in aircraft. Like almost any other pilot I knew little about this and simply noted that the subject of metal fatigue had been quoted as a factor in numerous accidents and incidents. I decided that perhaps it was a subject which merited a bit more awareness by aircrew and, working on the principle that the other pilots in the Air Force were just as ignorant as I was, I went up into our technical library and sorted out everything I could find on the subject, which in those days was not a lot. I then took these back to my office and slowly read them all. I understood some of it and after a second reading I understood a bit more. That was when the trouble started. I picked up my pen and my paper, and I started to write. Slowly, very slowly the volume of information built up – no danger of my pen suffering from metal fatigue – and after about a solid week of writing and rewriting I came up with around 5,000 words on the subject. This went to the typist as a first draft and then using well tested techniques, I tried it out on the other members of the directorate. This resulted, as usual, in several suggested amendments and the second draft took form. Finally I decided that it was about as good as I was going to get it, and it went for its final typing. The procedure which we used was to circulate such papers to the real experts to ensure that we were not putting out any duff information so, among other destinations, one copy went to the Royal Aircraft Establishment at Farnborough. A few days went by and then I was called into the office of the Director of Flight Safety.

'What have you been up to Rufus?' he asked.

'Nothing special, sir, I replied. 'Why?'

'Farnborough want you down there right away,' he told me. So without delay I caught a train and on arrival I found myself ushered into the office of the Director of RAE. 'I have just been shown the article you wrote on metal fatigue for aircrew,' he said. 'My chaps have been trying to write that paper for the last five years but they can't manage it.'

'They wouldn't sir,' I replied. 'They all know too much about it and would get snarled up in too much scientific jargon. I wrote this as an ignorant pilot for other ignorant pilots. I worked on the basis that if I could understand it then any other pilot could understand it.' To cut a long story short, I spent a fascinating day down there and the real stress experts showed me some of the work they were doing and we went through my article together in great detail. Strangely, very few changes were needed. In due course, the next issue of *Air Clues* came out and there in the centre was my article on Metal Fatigue in Aircraft. I had discussed it with our artist, Norman Atwill, and he had provided a lovely set of illustrations for me and even I was quite pleased with it when I saw it in print. Within a few days, both BOAC and BEA had been on the phone, asking if they could reprint it in their house magazines and I also I noticed that the Society of Licensed Engineers and Technologists had reprinted it in their house magazine. The next thing that happened to my article was that the Flight Safety Foundation in America printed it in full in a special issue and it became the definitive article on metal fatigue for aircrew world wide. Altogether a very satisfying conclusion to a heck of a lot of work. It is a pity it was 'Crown Copyright' or I might have made something out of it.

I'm sure it could have been a result of working in the unhealthy atmosphere of London, but in the middle of May 1964 I woke up one Saturday morning and got up as usual. I got my son, aged just under two years old, out of bed and dressed and then went downstairs to make breakfast. Something was definitely wrong. I felt like a bit of chewed string and I kept having to sit down before I fell down. After breakfast I went to see my GP and within an hour I was in St Thomas's Hospital having been diagnosed as having had a spontaneous pneumothorax (a collapsed lung to you). Eventually I came out of the Edward the Seventh Hospital at Midhurst in Sussex to which I had been transferred, just in time for Christmas. While I was there they performed 'the second most painful operation' on me. A thing called a pleuradhesis. In this they sprayed silver nitrate on the inside of my chest cavity to deliberately burn it so that my lung would stick to the fluids which resulted from the burn. Yes, it was just about as unpleasant as it sounds. I was grounded for a year after this operation but then they gave me back an unrestricted medical, so I suppose it was worthwhile in the long run.

When I had completed my time in the Ministry of Defence and had got my medical back, I was posted as CO of No. 4 AEF based at Exeter. This was an Air Experience Flight which provided flying for the Air Training Corps and the Combined Cadet Force in south-west England. My parish stretched from Land's End to Bristol and from Bristol to Weymouth I was there for several years and flew an awful lot of flights – about 6000 separate sorties.

Shortly after I arrived at Exeter and before I had taken over as the CO, Dickey Dougan, the outgoing boss, and I were scheduled to fly the aircraft over to RNAS Yeovilton to give Air Experience Flying to the boys from Sherborne College. We took off and, on arrival at Yeovilton, we found that the weather was nothing like the forecast. (This is a not unknown situation.) The wind was reported as being from 'three o'clock at 40 knots and gusting'. This is well over the maximum permitted wind speed for operating Chipmunks even when it is straight down the runway. As it was, with the wind at right angles to the runway meant that we would have had something like 40 degrees of drift on landing. The result would have been inevitable. So we told them that we would not be landing but would be returning to Exeter. When we flew down the runway, the drift angle looked horrendous and we then departed to the west. After a few miles we found some low cloud had formed and so we turned left and flew approximately due south until we reached the coast somewhere just east of Lyme Regis. Here we dived over the cliffs and followed them all the way back to Exmouth. There was sea fog which was lifting up over the cliffs, and this left a triangle of clear air just below the cliff into which we inserted our aircraft. I thought it a bit strange when I noticed a guy looking down on us as he fished from a breakwater. I just hoped that Dickey Dougan who was leading our formation knew what he was doing. When we reached Exmouth we turned into the Exe Estuary and, keeping to the right-hand side, continued until we reached the mouth of the River Clyst. Here we lined up parallel to the first stretch of the river because we knew that this put us on track for the western edge of the airfield. We got there just as another aircraft was carrying out a missed approach after failing to get any visual reference and it passed over the top of me at about 300 feet. I could hear it but I couldn't see it. We then did a smart about turn and landed on the disused runway, which we knew was clear and was adequate for our light aircraft. All our fuel gauges were reading nearly empty, so it was as well that we managed to get in on the first attempt. Some people might wonder why we didn't climb up into the cloud and come back at a nice safe height, for an instrument approach on arrival. The answer is that firstly the Chipmunk was not cleared for flight in cloud and secondly, with no navigation aids at all, we would have been dependent on a radar approach terminating at two miles. We would have been at 650 feet at that point and the cloud base was around 50–100 feet. I'm sure I don't need to enlarge on that. Incidentally, the forecast was for a reasonable day with good visibility but as so often happens in aviation, they got it wrong.

Every summer, the Chipmunks were deployed to a summer camp at an RAF station. One year I got a phone message to say that one of my aircraft was being ferried home because the engine ran so badly. When it arrived, I interrogated the ferry pilot who brought it back and he told me that it was 'dreadful'. There was a lot of vibration at almost all power settings and they had tried everything they could think of to correct it, to no avail. The aircraft was pushed into the hangar where our own engineers proceeded to check everything again. Valve timing, ignition timing, mixture settings, you name it, they reset it. Nothing at all was omitted. But still the engine ran like a bag of nails.

The engine fitter came to see me. 'I don't know what else to do, sir,' he said 'I have tried everything and I can't find a thing wrong with it but still it runs dreadfully badly.'

'I'll come and have a look at it,' I replied. 'You never know but a non-technical guy might spot something.'

He didn't look too optimistic but we walked over to the hangar. About 35 yards from the aircraft I stopped.

'I can tell you what the problem is,' I said, 'the propeller is in the wrong place.'

'Don't be daft, sir,' he replied. 'There is only one place you can put it.'

So I offered to show him. Having first made sure that the ignition switches were off, the fuel was off and the slow running control was in 'cut out' I asked him to hand swing the propeller. I set the propeller ready for him and he took

114

hold and gave it a pull and fell through the propeller arc. He got up looking more than a bit puzzled. That had never happened to him before, so I set it up again and once more he fell through the propeller arc. Now I had got him intrigued. I asked him to think of the position of a propeller when the engine stops. There is normally one blade between the one o'clock and two o'clock position. but on this aircraft when we approached it I noticed that the blades were at right angles to the usual position. He took my point, the propeller was removed and the hub dismantled completely. Then it was re-assembled and the propeller re-fitted – correctly this time. The engine started and ran as sweet as a nut. When they checked the technical records, they found that there had been an oil leak from the front of the crankshaft about a week earlier and the propeller had been removed for a new seal to be fitted. They must have done it wrong somehow because there is a master spline on the hub which should make it simple to re-assemble and impossible to fit incorrectly. Sometimes the most complex technical problems have a simple non-technical explanation, which can only really be spotted by a non-technical guy.

One day a new pilot arrived to join me at Exeter. He was an RAF pilot who had been co-pilot on Valiant aircraft and he was waiting for a captain's course. He had been attached to me for six months and as usual I showed him round the place and then sat him down to read the local Flying Order Book. When he had finished, and signed it as having read and understood it, we went flying in order to have a look at the local flying area, to show him the local procedures and to enable me to confirm that his flying was up to standard. He had recently been checked out on a Chipmunk at his home base and he told me that there were no problems. We went up to a reasonable height so that I could check his aerobatics and that sort of thing and then, since we were at about 6,000 feet I asked him to demonstrate to me a spin to the right and a recovery which I told him to initiate after two full turns. He pointed out that he had just been checked out on spinning and didn't need to do it again. Nevertheless I insisted. So he went into a spin to the right with the normal control inputs of full-right rudder and full-up elevator. After two turns he announced that he was 'recovering now'. I watched full left rudder go on and then the control column moved to the fully forward and fully left position. The aircraft continued to spin.

'This one is a bit slow recovering, sir,' he said.

'Carry on,' I replied. He continued, and the aircraft continued to spin.

'It's not going to recover,' he said.

'It won't if you persist with full left aileron,' I replied. The aileron was rapidly centred and the spin ceased almost at once. The aircraft was returned to a climb and I pointed out that the height was now 1,500 feet. We returned to 5,000 feet and on the way I discussed his recovery technique.

He was well over six feet tall and when he tried to recover, he had pushed the control column straight from the shoulder. So I asked him if his arms were both the same length.

'Of course they are,' he replied.

'OK then,' I said, 'in future whenever you spin, put both hands on the control column and you are bound to push it straight forward without any aileron application.' So we levelled out and he did as I had said; and it recovered cleanly every time.

After landing I hauled him into the office and we discussed the flight. I told him that I was not at all happy. He agreed that his spin recovery had been incorrect but he insisted that he had it all sorted out now. I told him that I didn't care a fig about that as it was an easy thing to correct. What I was thoroughly cross about was the fact that he had just read the Flying Order Book and in that book it says quite clearly that if an aircraft shows no sign of recovery from a spin at 3,000 *he is to bale out (with his cadet).* 'Why didn't you?' I asked. He had no answer. Don't worry, I told him, I would have stopped you, but if you are flying with a cadet and you don't bale out at 3,000 feet, you will have killed him as well as yourself.' I think he got the message that Flying Orders are just that, and he has no discretion in such a case.

Once or twice a year I used to go over to RAF Chivenor with one of the Chipmunks to do some glider towing for the Air Training Corps who operated five gliders from there. The Chipmunk is not the world's greatest glider tug but it copes somehow. There was a requirement for the Instructors at the RAF Gliding Centre to be current in aero-tow techniques and this was the annual occasion when we got them up to scratch. It made a pleasant day out for me. We usually got a nice sunny day, and the ATC Cadets were all as keen as mustard. On one such occasion, there were five gliders in operation, one Sedberg and four Cadets. The Sedburg was a bit heavy for towing with a Chipmunk but we could manage to get it up OK if the glider pilot flew it smoothly. On this particular occasion, the Chivenor-based Hunters were away on a detachment somewhere, but they were due back that evening. When the time approached for me to leave, I got airborne with the Sedburg and we carried out a very gentle right turn which took us over the small town of Braunton. I was delighted to notice that we suddenly went from a climb of around 100 feet per minute to a climb of 500 feet per minute. Once I had got clear of the thermal, I started a slow dumb-bell turn to take me back over roughly the same track and I'm glad to say, I found the thermal again and immediately signalled the glider to 'cut'. This he did and I dropped back down to the airfield, where the first Cadet glider was hooked on. I at once went to the same spot, where the Sedburg was circling and released the Cadet. This procedure I repeated three more times until I managed to get all five gliders into the thermal. I dropped the last tow rope and returned to Exeter. The next day the glider people phoned me.

'Many thanks for yesterday,' they said, 'we managed to get them all up to over 4,000 feet in that thermal after you left, but then the Hunters returned and we all had to land. That thermal was still going strong at 6 pm and I reckon that we would have made about 6,000 feet. That was the first time we have found such a thermal for years. I wondered if you would notice it, when we went through it the first time. Anyhow, thanks a lot.'

The other bit of glider towing which I also used to do involved the Sedberg glider and the Exeter Air Day. Normally I would go over to Chivenor early in the morning on the day of the show and tow the glider back to Exeter. We would do an aero-tow demonstration in the afternoon for the benefit of the airshow crowd and then in the evening, I would take the glider back to Chivenor. One year when we left, the weather was slowly getting worse and the wind was from the north-west. This gave us a down draft in the lee of the hills just north-west of the airfield and when we took off to return to Chivenor, I gather that the people in the crowd were taking bets as to whether we would clear the hills. I was a bit doubtful myself but we scraped over with about 150 feet to spare. When we landed at Chivenor, the glider pilot told me that he was far more worried than I was because he was flying below my slipstream and there were no fields there into which he could have flown if he needed to jettison. A least we gave the crowd something to talk about.

Three or four times a year, we used to take the Chipmunks down to St Mawgan to provide Air Experience Flying for the Cornwall Wing of the Air Training Corps. On one such occasion, the cadet who had joined me in my aircraft asked to go and have a look at where a small tanker had run aground the previous year. This was no problem and we duly went to that particular rocky inlet and examined the wreckage. As we were leaving, the cadet commented, 'That was a jolly big shark wasn't it, sir?'

'What shark?' I replied. 'I didn't see one.'

'Just off the wreck,' he replied, 'about 30 yards out.'

'Let's have a look,' I said, turning the aircraft round. We didn't have far to go and when the cadet pointed out the 'shark'. I laughed. 'That's a line of rocks on the seabed,' I told him. 'Anyhow it's far too big to be a shark, it must be at least 20–25 feet long.'

We flew low over the 'shark' and I prepared to return to St Mawgan. As we did so, 'the rocks' waved their tail out of the water. I was somewhat shaken, and mortified that he had recognised it as a very large shark and I hadn't. We watched it for a while as it cruised slowly north towards Trevose Head. Half a mile further up the coast was a delightful sandy bay, full of holidaymakers. Many of them were in the water swimming and one or two were further out playing with small surfboards. It struck me that the shark would get there in about 15 to 20 minutes. We set off to go back to St Mawgan and on the way, I discussed the shark with my cadet. Neither he nor I knew if such sharks were dangerous to humans. We landed uneventfully and as I taxied in, I called the Tower and asked them to phone the ground crew and have an airman ready to sit in the aircraft for a couple of minutes. When we parked, the airman was there waiting so I was able to get out and leave him temporarily in charge while I hurried over to the ground-crew hut. Here I picked up the phone and dialled the operator. I asked her to connect me with the police in Newquay. She wanted to know who I was and whether I was authorised to make outside calls. I gave her my name and rank and told her that I was visiting aircrew. So she declined to put me through. I refused to let her frustrate me and so I used a particular phrase with which she could not argue and she put me through at once. I spoke to a very nice police sergeant in Newquay and explained that I had observed this very large shark heading towards the bay full of people swimming, and I didn't know if it was dangerous, but if it was then the people should be told. I left it to him to decide and like me, he took the cautionary option. I returned to my aircraft and got in. Naturally the next cadet wanted to go and look at the shark. So we headed back to that area. When we got there I was relieved to see that there was a police car on the beach with its blue light on and a hoard of bathers clustered round the edge of the water. But no one actually in the water. The shark was slowly working its way round the bay, still heading north and minding its own business. I later found out that such large basking sharks are no danger to people as they only eat tiny plankton-like food, which they strain through filters in their mouth. Nevertheless, if I had been swimming in that bay and I had found a very large shark near me I would have had what I can best describe as an 'anti-social accident'. If I had later found out that someone had seen it and done nothing about it, I would have been a bit miffed to say the least.

In August 1969 I was attached to RAF Lindholm in Yorkshire running a summer camp for ATC cadets. They had five Chipmunk aircraft and I and several other pilots were there to provide Air Experience flying. The camp had only been running for three days when OC Flying sent for me and told me that I was needed urgently at Chivenor, as a witness into a fatal flying accident. When asked how long it would take me to get there, I replied: 'About two hours if I can take an aircraft, sir.'

He seemed to think that this was a good idea, so off I went. The next day, having given my evidence to the accident Inquiry, I set off back to Lindholm. It was one of those days when even the seagulls are walking. The radio was unnaturally silent as I flew north and eventually I was able to contact Shawbury where I was due to refuel. They gave me a radar approach through some atrocious weather and I finally came out of the bottom of the cloud at about 200 feet, in heavy rain. Having landed, to my astonishment, I was marshalled right into an empty hangar, where I stopped the engine and got out.

'We thought you would prefer to be in the dry, sir,' said the airman who had directed me there. The fuel tanker arrived and the refuelling was completed inside the hangar. This was strictly against the normal regulations but the hangar was totally deserted, there being nothing else at all, anywhere in the building, apart from me and my aircraft. After refuelling was complete, I restarted the engine and taxied out into the rain. Back at the runway, I took off and climbed slowly to 5,000 feet on track to RAF Finningley. Finningley is, or rather it was, the controlling airfield for the clutch of airfields and as such they organised inbound traffic to both airfields. After a while I gave them a call. Having established contact, the lady on the radio asked me how far I estimated I was from Finningley.

'About 45 miles' was the answer.

'Roger,' she replied, 'you are indicating overhead. Descend to, and maintain, 1,500 feet on a pressure setting of 988 millibars.'

'Do you mind if I don't?' I replied. 'The hills round here are 2,500 feet high.'

There was a pause then a different voice came on the air. 'Delta Yankee Foxtrot 65 [that was my callsign]. Do not descend; I say again; do not descend. Acknowledge!'

'Don't worry,' I replied, 'it was so damned dangerous, I wasn't going to!'

I carried on at five thousand feet and some 20 minutes later I was given a couple of heading changes to confirm identification and was told: 'Delta Yankee Foxtrot 65, you are now identified four miles west of Finningley, descend to 1,500 feet on 988 millibars, and contact Lindholm on 324.5 mhz [or whatever the frequency was].' I acknowledged the message and started to descend. Just before I changed frequency, a female voice came back on the air.

'Sorry about the earlier mix up DYF 65 but when you said 45 miles, I thought you had said four to five miles and you weren't pulling a trace on the VDF.'

'Don't worry,' I answered, 'it was so dangerous that it was really quite safe.'

In due course I landed and thought no more about it. The following Saturday, I had been out visiting an old friend of mine near York. I got back to the Mess at about 10.30 and decided to go straight to my room. I was intercepted on the way.

'Rufus, your air traffic lady is in the bar and she's hiding behind the pillar out of the way. She's terrified that you are going to start a row or something,' he said.

I couldn't resist it. I went into the bar and there she was. Her husband was at the bar getting some drinks, so I leant round the pillar and said: 'Excuse me. I think you owe me a drink.'

'What do you mean?' she replied.

'Delta Yankee Foxtrot 65,' I answered.

'Oh, s***!' she said in a loud voice. Husband returned instantly and wanted to know what was going on. She rapidly told him to get me a pint of beer. As soon as it arrived, I took a slurp and looked at her. 'OK, we are friends again now! Cheers!'

Once upon a time ... there was a pilot who flew Chipmunks with me at Exeter and who used to fly a Spitfire in the Second World War. Like all of us, he had a birthday each year. Now it came to pass that his wife went to London to do some shopping and as she arrived at the station to come home, there was the tail of the train vanishing into the dusk at the far end of the platform. She said something – history does not record what – and realising that she had to wait an hour for the next train, she wandered out of the station. After walking a short distance, she noticed one of those modern shops which specialises in cards for all occasions and remembering her husband's imminent birthday, she went in and spoke to one of the assistants.

'It's my husband's birthday in a few days and he used to fly Spitfires during the war. I don't suppose that you have a card with a picture of a Spitfire on it have you?' she asked him.

'I don't know, madam,' he replied, 'if you would like to take a seat, I'll have a look in the storeroom to see if I can find one.'

He was away for at least 20 minutes and when he reappeared, somewhat dusty, he had a solitary card in his hand. 'I've only been able to find this one,' he said, 'I'm afraid that it's not a particularly "birthday" type of card but I should think it is about the last card in London with a Spitfire on it. I only spotted it because it had slipped down between two boxes.'

'Never mind,' was the reply, 'I'll take it anyhow.'

She placed it in her bag and returned to the station. In due course she arrived home and, when the great day arrived, her husband appeared for breakfast, and there propped against his boiled egg, was a card. Inside was a picture of a Spitfire side on, drawn in pen and ink with a white background. A huge grin spread over his face. 'Gosh, that's wonderful,' he said. 'Who drew it for you?'

'Nobody,' was the answer, 'I got it in London when I was up there the other day. It's not very good but it was the only Spitfire picture I could find.'

'Rubbish!' he said, 'come clean and let me know who drew it. I want him to draw me a larger one which I can frame.'

'Honestly, I bought it in London,' she insisted. It looked as though there was going to be a situation developing.

'I may be simple,' he said, 'but do you really expect me to believe that you went into a shop and bought what you say

123

is probably the last Spitfire card in London and you just happened to get one with a picture of the very same aircraft that I flew on Ops in the war?' But she had.

Eventually, my masters at the Ministry of Defence decided that I had been at Exeter for long enough. I managed to persuade them to send me to RAF Chivenor as I wanted to keep my children in the same schools. Chivenor was the Operational Conversion Unit for the single-engine fighter force and operated Hunter aircraft. My particular job there was as OC the Hunter Emergency Section where I was responsible for the training in emergency procedures of all the staff pilots and the students. Fortunately they also had some Meteor and Chipmunk aircraft so I was able to get plenty of flying in all three types.

6

Ground Jobs: 1973–80

Chivenor
RAF Chivenor must be one of the most popular postings in the Royal Air Force. In those days the buildings were all wartime wooden huts and the morale and spirit of the whole station was terrific. I found that I was billeted in the same hut that I had been billeted in in 1950. It had been redecorated (probably more than once) but apart from the addition of electric heaters, there was very little difference.

Since my work at Chivenor consisted, in the main, of training the staff and students in the arts of survival, I had to go to RAF Mountbatten to the School of Combat Survival and Rescue to complete the Combat Survival and Rescue Officers Course. This is a pretty tough course consisting of several days' lectures, at least three liferaft drills and a week surviving on Dartmoor in midwinter. The cold/wet conditions make this one of the most environmentally unfriendly places one can imagine. We were wet to the skin most of the time and we had to work pretty hard on very short rations. The night navigation was a bit of a trick as there are many holes on the moor just waiting for the unwary 'survivor' to fall in. Every pace had to be probed in advance and it can come as quite a shock to find that you are trying to walk

125

straight off the edge of a quarry in pitch black conditions with steady rain and a very strong wind. It certainly concentrates the attention. The final phase of the exercise consists of a night escape and evasion task with very fit Royal Marines trying to locate and capture us. They have the advantage of night vision goggles and such items so, as you would expect, most people are caught. They are then treated like genuine POWs and after a while they are taken to one of the forts above Plymouth where they are subjected to intensive interrogation by the professional interrogators from the Army. Details of this treatment are classified so I won't go into details except to say that it is extremely unpleasant. In my own case I regained consciousness to find two doctors working on me after I had had a coronary arrest. I could put up with that but when I was reviving, the senior doctor asked me my age. When I told him, he asked me what the hell I was doing on the course as I was '15 years over the age limit'. 'Now you ruddy well tell me,' I replied. He decided that I was recovering OK.

For the necessary liferaft training, we used the Appledore Lifeboat. Almost every Wednesday, a coachload of students or staff went round to Appledore and we boarded the lifeboat. The boat then set off into Bideford Bay and when well out to sea, the students (or staff) were hurled into the sea and told to get into a liferaft and carry out all the standard drills. Later, the Chivenor helicopter would arrive on the scene and winch them out of their rafts and return them to Chivenor. The empty rafts were recovered by the boat which returned them to the shore where they were loaded on to the coach and taken home. I usually arranged to be picked up by the helicopter and flown back as it saved time. Sometimes they would winch me off the deck of the boat and sometimes if it was very rough I would leap into the sea and get picked up from there. Jumping ahead to my last week at Chivenor, I had gone over to Appledore as usual with a party of students. The liferaft drill had gone without a hitch but I noticed that the lifeboat crew were in a bit of a hurry. After we had collected the empty liferafts. I prepared myself for winching off the deck and asked the coxswain of the lifeboat if the helicopter wanted to winch me off the bows or the stern. He told me the stern was the place but, after a few seconds while the helicopter positioned itself off to one side, he poked his head out of the wheel-house and told me that they had changed their mind and wanted me off the bows. I set off forward and two of the crew came out of the wheel-house as I came by. One turned towards the bow and the other towards the stern. I was between them. The guy behind me then turned round and pinioned my arms while the one in front of me turned and grabbed my feet. About three seconds later I found myself propelled up and away from the boat. I hit the water with arms and legs flailing and when I resurfaced, I turned towards the lifeboat to find the entire crew lining the side and saluting. I got a different kind of salute from the helicopter crew who nearly fell out of their machine, they were laughing so much. The lifeboat then motored off and the helicopter dropped me a strop, and winched me up. The lifeboat crew were a nice bunch of guys.

It was not long after I had arrived at Chivenor that I became an example of what 'stress' can do to the human brain. I had been doing some circuits and bumps in the Chipmunk, using the short runway while the Hunters used the long runway. My radio call sign was 'Chipmunk 13' and I had completed three or four circuits. As I climbed away for the next circuit, the engine decided to pack up. I turned into a position from which to land and transmitted the usual 'Mayday' distress call. I flew the aircraft in a fairly tight orbit and called 'finals' only to be told by Air Traffic to 'Overshoot, we have an emergency!' This left me a bit nonplussed so I landed anyhow on 'my' runway, dodging the crash wagons which were going the other way towards the main runway. This stimulated a burst of rhetoric from the Air Traffic

Controller which slowly died away as he noticed that my propeller was stationary. In a slightly puzzled tone of voice, he called me and said, 'Chipmunk 13, did you used to have a different callsign?'

'Yes,' I replied 'I used to be Delta Yankee Foxtrot 65. Why?'

'Ah! that explains it. That was the callsign of the aircraft with an engine emergency,' they answered. I apparently reverted under stress to the old familiar callsign, rather than the new one, and then changed back when the immediate panic had subsided. It cost me a round of drinks for the Air Traffic crew that evening.

At Chivenor we had an Army Liaison officer permanently based with us and the guy who was in office when I got to Chivenor, had recently returned from a stint in Northern Ireland. One day his wife phoned him and told him that a parcel had arrived for him from Northern Ireland. He was a bit surprised as he was not expecting anything. When asked, his wife described the parcel as a large biscuit tin. The sort which is almost a cube. There was nothing on the parcel to indicate who has sent it and she asked if he wanted her to open it. Definitely not, was the immediate answer. He told her to put it in the garden shed and leave it there. As soon as she had hung up, he contacted his Army headquarters and discussed the parcel with the security guys there. They agreed with him that it should be treated as suspicious and they would send a disposal team to his house. When they all met there, the team looked at the parcel and decided that it should be classed as a potential dangerous package. They took it into the middle of the field at the back of his house, where they ran a bead of plastic explosive round the top. Retiring to a safe distance they remotely fired the charge and with a sharp crack and a puff of smoke the lid went flying up into the air. When the dust had settled, they went forward and the demolition expert reached into the box and extracted a card which he handed to the addressee. I don't know the exact words but they were along the lines of 'Dear Jim, I thought you would like the enclosed glass decanter which I found in Ireland recently. Regards, Tom.' When he looked into the box, to his amazement, he found that the decanter was completely undamaged. The 'expert' who had been sent to check it over had managed to blow off the lid without even cracking the glass decanter inside. I hope he was offered a dram, or two, before he left.

After I had been at Chivenor for about a year, I got a phone call from my wife who was at home in Sidmouth with the family. 'The kitchen is on fire. What shall I do?'

'Ring the fire brigade,' I replied, 'and unless it's a small fire, get yourself and the children out of the house.' I then got into my car and drove home to find the majority of the ground floor smelling of smoke and all the ceilings blackened. It had been a small fire – the traditional chip pan, but after speaking to me, my wife had smothered it with a rug and then evacuated the building until the fire brigade arrived. They made sure that there was no further danger and went home. The children were treating it all as a bit of an adventure but my wife was treating it as a major disaster. She was thinking of all the work she would have to do, cleaning up. But she cheered up when I reminded her that we were properly insured. It took several weeks to get the smell of burnt fat out of the house.

Our political masters decided that the unit should relocate at RAF Brawdy in South Wales. As soon as the contractors had got things well underway, I got asked to run a shuttle to, firstly Haverfordwest aerodrome and later to Brawdy, ferrying over guys who needed to take over buildings or oversee changes which were needed. It took about an hour each way in the Chipmunk but about six hours in a car, so it made sense to fly, but the Chipmunk is hardly the best aircraft for that job. I often wondered why the RAF didn't hire an Aztec or something similar, and take parties of five over at once. It would have made life a lot easier for me.

When the time came for the actual move, a mass of small railway trucks were provided and the RAF decided to pack them themselves. Packing containers is a very skilled job and as a result a very large proportion of the equipment was broken on arrival in Brawdy. I'm sure that the replacement equipment cost a great deal more than the cost would have been to employ professional packers. I didn't go with the unit to Brawdy, instead, I went to RAF Mountbatten.

Mountbatten

RAF Mountbatten was the home of the RAF School of Combat Survival and Rescue. I had been down here earlier when I had to complete the Combat Survival and Rescue Officers Course (CSRO Course) so I was able to fit into their organisation without too much problem. The primary task of the school was to train all RAF aircrew in survival procedures and to give them practical experience of liferaft handling in the open sea. We normally used an identical raft to the one used by the students at their base, depending on what sort of aircraft they flew. The secondary task was to train CSROs who would then go back to their units and be responsible for the survival training of the crews on that unit. This training also included Escape and Evasion, and Resistance to Interrogation training. Finally we were also the unit which parented the trials of all new survival equipment and procedures. That was where I came in. Nearly all my time was taken up conducting trials but I did manage to carry out some of the routine training, in order to keep myself up to scratch. Some of the things we experienced might be of interest.

As I have mentioned, the RAF School of Combat Survival and Rescue at Mountbatten among other tasks, trained Combat Survival and Rescue Officers (CSROs). This was a very physical course which also included a number of lectures on both the equipment and the principles of survival. The CSROs completed three liferaft drills during their

130

training, one using single-seat liferafts, one using multi-seat liferafts and one indoor drill in a swimming pool using both single and multi-seat liferafts. Part of the aim was to teach the CSRO students the necessary drills for survival but also it was our intention was to teach them how to organise and run such drills themselves because, on return to their parent units, they would be responsible for all the survival training needed by their own crews. Also included in the land element of the course was a five-day practical exercise during which the students had to travel fairly long distances over inhospitable terrain. They were required to practise constructing shelters of different sorts using only what they would have with them following a bale out from their aircraft, and they had to live off the land (without breaking the civil law). As I explained earlier, this training was carried out during November, December and January on Dartmoor. Since the trainees were expending fairly large amounts of energy they got pretty hungry trying to live off the land and it was normal for them to put out night lines in some of the streams in an effort to catch a few of the small trout which abound in those waters.

By coincidence we had been carrying out a liferaft drill on the Wednesday of the week that one of the CSRO courses was out on the moor, and one of the instructors had caught a dogfish of about seven pounds. This unfortunate fish was carried up on to Dartmoor and to the general area where the CSRO course was located. Hunting in the local streams we found one of their night lines and with great care attached this large dogfish to the small hook. The following morning when the owner of the fishing line went to inspect his lines he was flabbergasted to find this fish, some two feet long, on his line. The stream is only about three feet wide so there was great speculation on how it managed to get so far upstream. The general view was that it had been chasing a small trout. Dogfish is, in fact, completely edible, however, the course students, remembering their training, refused to consume it because it has a 'skin' rather than 'scales'. They remembered that all fish with scales can be eaten but the poisonous ones have skins, so if in doubt don't eat a fish with 'skin'. It was a shame really that they should waste so much good food. They should also have realised that it was a salt-water fish which could not live in a fresh-water stream.

My primary job at Mountbatten was to carry out trials of all new Survival Equipment and Procedures before they came into Service use and during the course of these trials one or two amusing incidents occurred. One week I had arranged to test some life jackets which were fitted with an experimental automatic inflation device. The initial tests were to confirm the reliability of the system so, having prepared the half dozen or so jackets which had been supplied for the trial, I put them on, one at a time, and hurled myself off the side of the breakwater into the sea some 15 feet below. This gave me about the same entry speed as I would have experienced following a parachute descent. The jackets all inflated successfully and after each leap, I swam to the steps in the side of the breakwater, climbed out, took off my inflated jacket and put on another one in order to repeat the performance. When all six had been tested, we went back to my office/workshop and the staff were instructed to dry the jackets and re-arm them for another six leaps in the afternoon. Getting them dry took a long time and so we all adjourned for lunch. After our meal, there was another delay because the transport I needed was wanted for another job and it was well into the afternoon before we got back down to the breakwater, so we were running very late. The observers positioned themselves as before, and I put the first jacket on. Striding up to the edge of the breakwater, I launched myself. That's funny, I thought, I haven't hit the water yet! I continued to fall for what seemed like several minutes before hitting the sea with an almighty wallop which was followed by a thump on my feet as I hit the seabed. That's right, the tide had gone out and what had

Ground Jobs: 1973–80

been a 15-foot drop was now about a 35-foot drop. It was the sort of landing which brings a tear to one's eye and a lump to one's throat. I suppose I was lucky that there was sufficient water to break my fall. I shudder to think what would have happened if the tide had gone out another seven or eight feet, far enough to reach the sand and rock which make up the seabed just there. The observers thought this was all hilarious but somehow I just didn't see the joke. Needless to say, once I had got my breath back, I went off a platform lower down the steps for the five remaining leaps.

Another of the more restful trials which I had to carry out was a comparison of the 'old' type reflective tape which we used on the liferafts and a 'new' type which was under development. Among the various tests, I decided on a practical one, in which I intended to put two liferafts out in the sea and then search for them using the lights carried on a Search and Rescue Helicopter. One liferaft was fitted with the 'old' tape and the other with the 'new'. These were positioned off the beach near RAF Chivenor and when it got dark, we went off to search for them. We had only a rough idea where they had been put so we weaved up and down until we were able to pick up the liferafts by the reflection of the Whirlwind's landing light. In practical terms, the 'new' tape became visible at about double the range of the 'old' tape. This was very much what we expected from earlier trials on land and provided sufficient improvement to justify a change in the specification of the reflective tape on new liferafts. It also managed to get me a good hour and a half of night flying in the Whirlwind. Some people even had the temerity to suggest that the chance to fly a Whirlwind was the real reason for having the trial. What nonsense!

A more exciting trial involved research into the characteristics of being towed at high speed by a parachute after an automatic liferaft had deployed and to determine if a survivor could release himself from the parachute in these conditions. We could not rely on a real parachute to tow at the speeds we wanted so, as usual, we towed from the mast of a RAF launch. This gave the correct angle of tow and the speed could be controlled. We set off with me wearing the type of parachute worn by Phantom crews and with the launch making good about 18 knots down wind. This represented a wind effect in excess of 30 knots, as a parachute will tow a person in the water at about half wind speed. From my point of view it was an exciting rollercoaster ride. I was bounced from wave to wave, frequently submerging completely. The hardest part of the operation was removing the safety pins which inhibit premature release but once I had managed this – mostly by Braille – I was able to release the harness fittings and allow the boat to go on its way while I pulled in my liferaft and boarded it to await 'rescue' by the launch. I was a bit disturbed to find that the sea anchor had broken away during the high-speed dragging through the water. This made the liferaft totally unstable and liable to be rolled over every time a wave smacked into the side of it. There were still about four feet of string left where the drogue had been attached so I removed my flying helmet – known in the Air Force as a 'bone dome' – and tied the chin strap to the broken painter. Casting this overboard, I was relieved to find that it worked just as well as the original sea anchor and stabilised the liferaft nicely. Then the launch tried to come alongside and pick me up, and that's when the fun started. The normal technique was to catch the drogue painter with a boat hook and pull the raft close enough for the 'survivor' to clamber aboard. In this case, the very rough sea and the abnormally short painter made this a somewhat hazardous manoeuvre. After they had hit me twice with the boat hook, they backed off to think about it. The next attempt was significantly worse. This time as the launch closed with me, it was caught by a very large wave and carried completely over the top of my raft. When I resurfaced I found that the launch was now on my starboard side. It had been on the port side when it approached. Fortunately the guy in charge of the launch decided that this was getting ridiculous. He backed off and called out the SAR helicopter from Culdrose. By the time it arrived, some 25 minutes later, I had drifted well into the naval weapons range, at HMS *Cambridge*, but they were not firing that afternoon. As soon as the helicopter arrived, they lowered a winch man who was able to use a 'snatch' technique as they trawled him past me. This involves hooking on to the handholds on the front of my life jacket with a hook. When the weight comes on to these handles, the stitching all rips causing the 'survivor' to feel that he is falling through the jacket, but it is designed that way and I was ready for the heart-stopping moment when you feel a ripping all across your back. One is literally dragged out of the raft, into the sea and the helicopter then lifts the winch man and the survivor clear of the water. This is not the normal rescue technique, which would have involved a strop and a much more comfortable ride, but it is used when the conditions are too bad for a strop lift. The helicopter dropped me on the ground at Mountbatten before returning to Culdrose. The raft was abandoned to make its own arrangements. All in all it was an exciting and invigorating ride. But we found out what we wanted to know about liferaft behaviour and the ability of a survivor to detach himself from a harness even under such extreme conditions.

One of the most difficult trials to organise involved testing the new (in those days) Pye Locator Beacon. This is a radio locator beacon which is fitted in every RAF life jacket. It is normally manually activated by survivors and assists the Search and Rescue aircraft to find them. To carry out a practical test of the beacon's capabilities (or otherwise) I arranged to be dropped in the sea some 50 miles from land. There I intended to inflate, and then board, a single-seat liferaft, activate my beacon, and await (hope for?) rescue. In the RAF there are several aircraft with an SAR role and it made good economic sense to test the beacon with all of them simultaneously. In consequence I made arrangements for one Nimrod, one Hercules, one Sea King, one Wessex and one Whirlwind to be tasked for this search at the same time. The Nimrod was to start at 30,000 feet, the Hercules at 10,000 feet, the Sea King at 5,000 feet, the Wessex at 2,000 feet and the Whirlwind at 1,000 feet. I also had one of the RAF High Speed Launches looking for me at sea level. The intention was that each aircraft would fly until he was out of range of the beacon and then turn and search for the beacon to establish the maximum range at which it could be detected. Each aircraft was to make one search into wind, one down wind and two cross wind to establish the shape of the transmission radiation. Having completed this, each aircraft was to descend one level and repeat the performance. So it took several hours.

You have no idea how lonely it can get sitting in a single-seat liferaft out of sight of land or indeed out of sight of any boats at all. The raft is about four feet long and two feet wide inside and there is no room to do anything but sit in it with your knees bent as it's too short to straighten your legs.

About three hours into the trial, I was somewhat disturbed to hear a hissing noise start up. My heart did a couple of twitches and I started to look for the leak. I got the leak stoppers out (threaded rubber cones to 'screw' into a leak or tear) and I plugged the hand bellows into the inflation point in preparation. I hunted everywhere but no matter how hard I tried, I could not find that leak. Finally I decided to tell the searching aircraft that I might need pulling out after all. So I reached on to the floor of the raft near my left buttock and picked up the beacon. The beacon is fitted with a 'speech' facility so that survivors can talk to rescue aircraft. When I picked my beacon up I found that the switch had been knocked to the 'receive' position and the hissing was from the loudspeaker. You can't imagine what a relief it was to find that my raft didn't have a leak! I returned the switch to the auto transmit position and relaxed. Strangely the Hercules was the only aircraft homing at that time. In their report they stated that they had picked up the beacon at 70-miles range and then, at about 60 miles, the beacon suddenly ceased – as though it had been turned off. They continued on their original heading and suddenly the beacon restarted when they reached 45 miles, and so they continued with the test. They were quite right in their diagnosis. It did, however, confirm that the switch was not nearly positive enough and a redesigned switch was fitted on the production beacons to ensure that such a *faux pas* couldn't recur.

Another amusing incident occurred when I got a phone call from RAF Boscombe Down. They were in the middle of some trials with a Sea King into which they had installed a new homing device. They were intending to put a liferaft out into the Channel and then to carry out a series of homings using the new equipment, but their 'training' beacon had broken and they couldn't do the job. They wanted to know if I had a 'training' beacon and if so, could I get someone out into the Channel to enable them to carry out their trial. Fortunately I had a 'training' beacon – crystallised on 245.1 mhz as opposed to the 'operational' beacon which is crystallised on 243 mhz. I was happy to arrange for one of our staff instructors to go out to mid Channel for them and so off went one 'volunteer', armed with a life jacket containing the 'training' beacon. In due course, when they had arrived in Lyme bay, he launched into the sea some 15 miles off the coast and switched the beacon on.

Meanwhile the Sea King had got airborne from Boscombe Down and was on his way to start the search when he was contacted by the London Distress and Diversion cell and asked to abort his trial and commence a real search for someone who had ditched in the Channel. So the Sea King set off on its new task and after a while, picked up the operational beacon, homed to it and lowered a winch man. Only to find my guy asking him why he was so late? The

137

'training' beacon, so-called, was switched off and the operational signal on 243 mhz died away. The situation was
explained to London D & D cell, who relaxed and gave them
the OK for the trial to continue using the so-called 'training'
beacon in spite of its operational frequency crystal. In due
course, the Sea King finished its task, and my guy was
picked up by the boat and returned to Mountbatten, where
he told me the sorry story and suggested that we didn't use
the 'training' beacon until it had been fitted with a 'training'
crystal. I agreed and started to get everything tidied up for
the night – it was just coming to five o'clock when everyone
hopes to knock off and go home. It suddenly struck me. If I
had a training beacon with a 243 crystal, where was the 245.1
crystal? Answer: it must be in an operational beacon somewhere. So taking a deep breath I contacted the Communica-
tions centre and told them not to close down as I had an
Operational Immediate signal to send in a few minutes.
About ten minutes later a signal was winging its way to
every flying unit in the Royal Air Force stating that somebody, somewhere probably had an operational beacon with
a training crystal fitted in error. All beacons were to be
frequency-checked before the next flight. I went home
having caused chaos in the whole of the Air Force. Next day,
the Ministry of Defence was on the phone wanting to know
what was going on. So I told them and they agreed (thank
goodness) that I had taken precisely the correct action. At
about 10.30 that morning I got a phone call from RAF
Binbrook, a Lightning flghter base. They had found a beacon
in a pilot's life jacket with a 'training' crystal fitted to it. I was
then able to send a second signal cancelling the first. 'That
which was lost has now been found – at Binbrook.' It's not
often that a relatively junior officer such as I can ground the
whole of the Air Force and get away with it.

I also managed to achieve distinction one day by grounding all the Tornado aircraft. I was carrying out the final trials
of the full assembly carried by the Tornado pilots. This

consisted of a new parachute, which was excellent, a new liferaft which was excellent, a new life jacket which was excellent, a new seat harness which was excellent and sundry other minor elements which were also both new and excellent. This final series of trials consisted of a simulated parachute entry into the water with a moderate wind of 20 knots. This involved towing the 'survivor' from the mast of a boat to reproduce the pull of the new parachute. To my dismay I found that when all the elements were put together, they were totally lethal and there was no way a survivor could live if he baled out into the sea in a 20-knot wind. The problem was that the new automatic liferaft inflated as the 'survivor' dropped into the sea. This rolled him face down and the parachute pulled him through the water. Being face down, he acted like a hydroplane and dived down deeper. Meanwhile the liferaft on its 20-foot connecting strop had filled up and was acting like a large sea anchor. This put a terrific strain on the parachute harness so that it was impossible to release from the 'parachute'. The pressure also meant that the survivor couldn't roll himself face side up, and so he slowly ceased to be a survivor. I found this rather frustrating. The guys on the boat didn't know what was going on as all they could see was a swirl from the liferaft and me as we were dragged through the water about seven feet below sea level. I had a chase boat formating some 20 yards from me, to film the performance and to be able to comment on what was going on. After a while, since they could see nothing, they sheered away. The towing boat saw this and realising that the trial was definitely not going as expected, they jettisoned the tow from their end. By now I had swallowed a great deal of salt water and was taking no interest in what was going on around me. The inflated life jacket popped me back to the surface and the boat, which had turned round, hauled me out of the sea, emptied the water out of me and bump-started my breathing again.

When I had got myself under control, I discussed the situation with my station commander, who had volunteered himself to join in as my assistant on the trial. We repeated the previous run but this time we agreed to jettison the tow after 20 seconds and, in the event, exactly the same problem happened to him so we jettisoned after 15 seconds. Naturally, the station commander accused us of keeping him under water for at least a minute – that's what it feels like. I did one more run with some minor changes to the parachute harness but it had no effect on the problem and when hauled back on board the boat, I turned to the CO and told him that: 'This trial is now terminated, because we are going to kill someone if we aren't careful.' He looked very relieved. 'Thank goodness for that,' he replied, 'it was my turn next.'

When I got ashore, I drafted my report and then had a long phone call with Johnny Squires the Chief Test Pilot at Warton where Tornados are built and where the initial test flying was taking place. Following my talk with him he informed me that he was grounding the Tornado from flight over water until this problem had been sorted out. In the event it took a couple of months and the 'cure' was found to be to fit water pockets on the rim of the parachute so that it tripped itself up if it tried to tow a survivor through the water.

For many years the RAF has used a survival compass which was the size of a very large wrist watch. These were very good compasses but were bulky and expensive. I decided that with modern technology we ought to be able to find something a bit better. So we contacted Silva Compasses to see what they had got. A box of alternative samples were sent down for me to look at. Most were sophisticated modern compasses used for orienteering or serious cross-country walking but they were much more bulky that the existing wrist compass. However, there was one other possibility. They had sent me a compass called a 'Huntsman'. This was a very small compass with a rotating bezel and a hinged flap which could be used to double the physical size of the compass. Helpful when laying off courses on a map, or it could be used at right angles to the magnetic part of the compass to enable bearings to be taken. In addition there was a pin clip which was available to enable the survivor to pin the compass to his chest so leaving both hands free for other duties. By pinning it to the front of the survivor's blouse and setting the required track on the bezel, he could maintain a course.

So what is a survival compass required to do? First it should enable the survivor to take bearings and so plot his position. Then it should enable him to measure the track he needs to follow to his destination and, thirdly, it needs to provide him with the ability to march along that track even in total darkness. Initially, therefore, I used the compass to take bearings of various points round Mountbatten. These I plotted on a large-scale map and I found that the bearings gave me a position some 15 yards away over the road outside my office. Near enough for government work, as they say. Next I measured several tracks and compared them with the actual bearings as determined by other means. Once more the compass was adequate. Finally I did a practical cross-country march using the compass.

For this part of the trial I drew a line from a trig-point on the map to a milestone some 15 miles away. I then measured the track very carefully and made all the necessary corrections for magnetic variation and for grid convergence. Accompanied by a friend (Ron Boxall) who is a great long-distance walker we were dropped off on the edge of Dartmoor and made our way to the trig-point. This is a concrete and steel plinth erected by the map makers and positioned very accurately indeed. We found that this put us well and truly in the clouds so there was no way we could cheat. We then set off using the compass to keep us on a dead straight line, for our milestone. It is a very slow business travelling cross country with a visibility of around

15 yards, if you are going to maintain an accurate compass course. We came to a river at one point and here, rather than wade across (it was several feet deep and very fast flowing) we put a marker down, headed upstream to a bridge, crossed over and returned to restart our march exactly opposite our 'marker'. Several hours went by and at last we reached the road on which our milestone should be. No sign of it. The nearest public house was to our right a few miles away so we naturally turned right. Some 20 yards from where we had reached the road I tripped over a milestone hidden in the long grass. Yes, it was the one we were aiming for. We agreed that after some six plus hours of cross-country walking, being 20 yards off track was not unreasonable. So we continued to the pub where we were able to ring Mountbatten and get them to send a vehicle to pick us up. We only had to wait about an hour so I expect we managed to sample the local brew.

On the whole the compass had performed well. It was sufficiently strong to withstand the forces of ejection from an aircraft and it cost about 15 per cent of the price of the 'old' wrist compass. So the RAF introduced the Silva Huntsman into every survival pack in preference to the previous wrist compass. Well done, Rufus, I thought. Don't you believe it! Some few years later, the Falklands War started and during that conflict one of the Harrier pilots had cause to bale out. He landed in open country and after unpacking his survival kit he tried to fix his position. The compass didn't work. Indeed it was utterly useless. So what went wrong? In the UK, the magnetic north pole lies, not in a straight line north of the observer but, in a downward pointing direction towards the north magnetic pole. In fact the angle of dip, as it is known, induces a 60 degree down pull on a compass. The Huntsman compass needle is counter balanced so that it lies flat and pivots in the horizontal plane in temperate latitudes in the Northern Hemisphere. I expect you have caught on by now. I used

Ground Jobs: 1973–80

the words 'Northern Hemisphere'. But the Falklands are in the Southern Hemisphere and 'dip' is in the other direction so the needles in 'my' compasses simply jammed hard against the glass and did nothing else. I had retired from the Air Force by this time so I don't know what the cure was. Probably something quite simple but I was disgusted with myself for not foreseeing this potential problem.

One of the more relaxed trials I had to carry out was on a new design of solar still. Shortage of water is often one of the main problems encountered in the survival world. Especially at sea where you are surrounded by millions of tons of the stuff all of which is undrinkable. Various methods have been tried to convert it to a drinkable quality, but the results have hardly justified the means. The solar still was an inflatable plastic device which used solar energy to evaporate sea water and then condense the vapour back into drinkable water. It was quite a neat design about one metre in diameter and light enough to be stowable in a liferaft pack. In order to test its ability to distil sufficient water I proposed to fly out to the Indian Ocean, to an island called Gan in the Maldive group of islands. This island was an RAF staging post to the Far East and the entire population was either RAF or RAF employed. Addu Atoll is a typical atoll with several islands round the rim of the reef and Gan was one of the larger ones. There was a very deep lagoon, full of fish, in which I was able to deploy a number of stills. They were tethered to a liferaft moored in the lagoon and twice daily we used to go out to the raft, pull in the stills and measure the volume of distillate. We also sampled it for taste. In addition to this, we also had half a dozen stills on land. Their reservoirs were filled with a variety of fluids and these too were emptied twice daily and sampled for taste. The results were quite good and all the stills remained fully inflated for the ten days that we were there. As expected those on land did slightly better than those in the lagoon because of the higher temperatures

143

giving more rapid evaporation. At the end of our stay, we flew back to the UK in a VC10, having five consecutive 'breakfasts' on the way. On arrival in England, my partner returned to his work and I was joined by an American Marine Officer for the second half of the trial in Gibraltar.

We flew to Gibraltar in an RAF Britannia aircraft and lived in the Mess there. The stills were deployed in the sea off the entrance to the RAF Marine Craft depot and we were ferried out twice daily to measure and sample the distillates. Again, all the stills worked well and the products were comparable with the output in the Indian Ocean. Once more we returned to the UK and in due course the samples were tested and declared 'potable'. In fact they were dreadfully bland and plasticy but if they are going to keep you alive in a water-short environment then who really cares about the finer points of taste?

There was much discussion on the value of strobes as opposed to steady lights and each side had its protagonists. I started with an open mind and we carried out a series of tests. One of these consisted of putting three guys out into the sea on a black night and seeing from how far away we could find the lights when we didn't know where they were. Previous tests had shown that when you know roughly where to look you could see the bright flash of a strobe well. On the night in question we had two guys in single-seat liferafts about a mile apart: one with a normal McMurdo light, which is a steady light with a water-activated battery, and the other with a strobe. A third survivor was put in the sea about three-quarters of a mile further on without a liferaft and with just a strobe on his life jacket. The CO of the School of Combat Survival and Rescue volunteered himself for that task. I was able to encourage him and the others by reporting that three record sharks had been caught in the previous 24 hours in the region where we were going to be: a Porbeagle, a Thresher and a Mako.

The observers searching for the survivors were in an RAF launch and only knew the general area to search. We started searching about five miles from the survivors and it was not until we were about one and a quarter miles from them that we managed to see first one, then the second, of the liferafts. We were within half a mile of the swimmer without a liferaft before we found him. There was really no practical difference in the range at which we spotted the rafts, the steady McMurdo light being just as good as the flashing strobe.

On another occasion two pilots had to bale out from a Lightning, into the North Sea off Scotland and the Rescue Helicopter picked them both up. In their reports these pilots said that they had the life-jacket lights on and in addition one had a strobe. He was an American officer on an exchange posting to the RAF and he claimed that he had been picked up first because he had a strobe. I studied the helicopter pilot's report. In it he remarked that he understood that one of the survivors had a strobe but he had not noticed which one it was so he couldn't comment on its efficiency.

In a third trial a nine-man liferaft was fitted with a strobe and was taken out and dropped in the Channel. The crew inside got so bored waiting for the searching Shackleton to find them that they sat down, lit three McMurdo lights inside the raft and had a game of cards. The report from the Shackleton said that they finally picked up the raft visually by the glow from the door. It was only when they got close that they realised that it was the raft with the strobe. After these trials and reports, I favour the steady light in preference to a strobe for visual acquisition of an object at night whose position is unknown.

One of the more energetic trials we carried out concerned a 30-man raft. After the usual righting and durability trials we got on to the max overload series. For this I needed a total of 45 people. This was rather more than I could find from Mountbatten resources so I borrowed a few from the Navy. They very kindly provided 30 young seamen to make up the numbers. These were not too happy at the thought of having to jump in the sea and swim to a raft and board it. I cheered them up a little by telling them that they would be issued with RAF immersion suits for the trial. Then I really put a smile on their faces when I remarked that the 15 RAF types in the crew included several members of the WRAF. The trial went off quite well and when it finished I had organised a Sea King helicopter to pick everyone up from the raft and ferry them back to Mountbatten. Having landed half the survivors, they came back to pick up the others. By the time the crew of the liferaft had been reduced to five or six, the raft was pretty light and floating well out of the water. The Sea King has a lot of rotor down-wash and the normal drill is to deflate the canopy and lie on top of it. This we did but to no avail. The raft, with five guys clinging to the top of the deflated canopy, was picked up and hurled out to sea, rolling over and over as it went. This was quite an exciting ride. Finally I decided that enough was enough so I pulled out my knife and stabbed the liferaft. This caused it to collapse and the helicopter was able to come and rescue the last few survivors. The escort boat salvaged the raft and took it home.

For some time there has been a view that an unconscious pilot who bales out over the sea will, provided he has been able to inflate his life jacket, be turned the right way up in the water but will then get tangled up in his parachute so may or may not be alive when picked up. I had a few doubts about this so I got permission to carry out a trial to see what really happened. For the trial I used a normal pilot-type harness, parachute, life jacket and survival pack. It was necessary to carry out the trial on an appropriately windy day and the water entry had to be exactly representative of a real parachute entry. When a suitable day arrived, I went out in one of the RAF launches and we

146

headed into the strong wind. I stood on the stern of the boat wearing all the kit and two other survival instructors held the parachute. They popped the parachute at a suitable moment and the result was that I was 'para-sailed' up to about 100 feet. Naturally I came back down again but by now the parachute had stabilised and I hit the sea exactly as I would in a descent from greater height. I didn't move because I was simulating an unconscious guy. After some three of four waves, I was turned over on to my back by the effect of the life jacket and I lay there in the water and waited to see what happened. It was not a bit like the theory we had been given. First the drogue bullet, a metal rod about 14 inches long, sank and this pulled down the drogue chute which remains attached to the top of the parachute. The waves going up and down caused the drogue to sink and this in turn pulled the parachute canopy down slowly. Since I, being on the surface, was going up and down under the influence of the waves and the parachute, below wave depth, stayed in a slow descent, the parachute opened and closed in time with the waves. It opened further each time until eventually it was fully open. Then it acted as a huge sea anchor attached to me by the parachute harness. As the waves came to me I could no longer go up and down because I had the weight of several tons of water in the parachute holding me down. The parachute was below the level of the waves in relatively still water but I was on (or near) the surface which was going up and down. So the waves rolled over me. I found that after two minutes' elapsed time, following my splash down, I was held under water for 75–80 per cent of the time. Had I really been unconscious, I would have drowned. As it was, I was able to hold my breath long enough to come up to the surface each time. I then signalled the launch to close with me and detached from the parachute. Once they had pulled me aboard, they had a very long pull to get the canopy to collapse so that they could get it out of the water. We repeated the test three times and got the same results every time. Our conclusion? If a parachutist bales out and goes unconscious before he can release from his parachute, then within a very few minutes he will drown if there is any sort of a sea running, and there almost always is. Over the years several unfortunate aircrew who had been found washed up on the beach, cocooned in their parachutes, had not been killed by being tangled up. They had almost certainly drowned when the parachute sank and kept them below water level for the majority of the time. The tangle in their parachutes occurred when they got rolled up and down the beach.

I spent several years at Mountbatten testing safety and survival equipment. There were a number of occasions when it didn't work out as forecast and there were times when it did. There were trials when it all got a bit hairy, but I had a really good team backing me up and anyhow when it didn't work out as we hoped, it was probably because I had done something wrong. However, it all became worthwhile on 3 June 1978. It was a Saturday morning and I had planned to go to Exeter, where I was due to fly with the Exeter Flying Club. I was just getting ready to leave my house in Plympton when the telephone rang. My wife, Olive, answered it. 'It's for you,' she said, 'it's the station commander from Mountbatten.'

I took the phone expecting to be told that I was required for duty or some such message. Not at all. He apologised for phoning so early, but he knew I was due to go to Exeter and he thought I would like to know that Her Majesty the Queen had seen fit to appoint me as a Member of the Most Excellent Order of the British Empire in her Birthday Honours list. It took a few minutes for it to sink in. He then added his personal congratulations. Olive was a bit speechless. I was in somewhat of a daze as I drove to Exeter later, and I don't think I gave the flying my full attention either. By the time I got home there were a number of messages from well-wishers. I was somewhat embarrassed on the following Monday when I found I was expected to be properly dressed and I had not had time to get the ribbon. That was cured by a quick visit to the RAF Stores, and that evening Olive rather enjoyed doing the necessary needlework. It was October before I got my summons to the Palace for the Investiture. What a day that was. To be honest I don't remember all the detail but I very distinctly remember the moment when I shook Her Majesty the Queen's hand and she pinned the Order on my uniform. The party afterwards in the RAF Club was quite a do. Most of the organisation was carried out by Olive, including getting my son, Nigel, collected from his school in Hampshire and ferried to London and back so that we were all there. It was an exhausting day to say the least, but I've got the traditional photographs of my family and me, outside the gates of Buckingham Palace, clutching my new medal, to remind me of a day which I can never expect to be repeated.

I found the several years I had spent at Mountbatten to have been very rewarding and full of that elusive factor 'job satisfaction' but all good things come to an end.

My 38 years spent in the Royal Air Force were a fascinating and exciting experience. I am not at all sorry that I missed the 'shooting' part of the war. I was extremely lucky to have had the chance to fly some of the most highly developed and efficient single-seat piston-engined fighter aircraft that have ever been invented and that I was able to take an active part in the development of the early jet fighters. If I was to be given the opportunity of serving for a different period I don't think I would change it by one day. I had a wonderful career in the Air Force and now that I fly civilian aircraft, mainly on training, I find a great deal of job satisfaction in trying to pass on a little of what I have learned.

7

Civil Aviation: 1980–93

The CAA

When I left the Royal Air Force, I was lucky enough to find immediate employment, with the Civil Aviation Authority. I worked for the Authority in the Flight Crew Licensing Directorate, where I spent a large proportion of my time dealing with 'approved' courses at various flying schools throughout the country. These had to be inspected every year, and so I would set off periodically on inspection rounds. As a result I soon got to meet many of the people involved in training pilots throughout the United Kingdom. At first it was a terrific culture shock moving from the world of an RAF officer, where everything is organised to run your life, to the world of a civilian where nothing is organised for you. My sister owned a flat in London which I was able to rent and I became a weekend commuter between London and Plymouth. As a result, I managed to put 100,000 miles on my car, a Citroën GSA, in only four years. Since it had been used only two days a week on Fridays and Sundays, it was in excellent condition when I traded it in for another Citroën – a diesel this time.

Generally speaking my time with the CAA gave me a very useful insight to the working of the Authority and also enabled me to make many contacts with senior people in the industry. It also gave me a good insight into some of the rackets and fiddles which people tried to take advantage of. One of the more interesting tasks which I was given was the drafting of the initial regulations regarding the flying of Microlight aircraft. Up to that time, they had been largely ignored by Authority, but obviously their activities would need to be regulated so that the general public were not put at risk. I managed to spend a couple of days with one of the larger Microlight Schools in Oxfordshire, where I had the opportunity of talking to instructors, students, pilots, engineers and the people in the neighbourhood. I also got the chance to fly a Microlight, which was interesting to say the least. When I returned to London, there was amazement in some quarters that I should have felt the need to talk to the operators before drafting the ground rules under which they would have to operate. Having spoken to them in depth, I was able to draft a fairly comprehensive set of regulations, almost all of which have stood the test of time and are still operative now, nearly 15 years later.

Another of my self-appointed tasks was to carry out a sort of devil's advocate job on the written examinations before they were issued, to ensure that both the questions and answers were as correct as we could get them. The guys who set the exams were too close to the trees to see the wood, and as a result I frequently found an answer or a question which was either incorrect or ambiguous. If it was possible to misunderstand a question then I would, and it would have to be reworded so that I couldn't.

In my day, the CAA offered monetary allowances, now eliminated, which were provided to enable members of the staff of the CAA who held aircrew licences to keep in current flying practice. This was a useful help and I normally used my training allowance to visit flying schools when I was carrying out an inspection. I thought it appropriate that a CAA official should fly himself to the various airfields he visited, even if only to show that he was not totally ignorant about aviation. I was also able to use this training allowance to carry out the necessary flying to enable me to obtain my professional pilot's licence. I had held a Private Pilot's Licence, with an Instructor Rating and Examiner Authority for several years, but my boss thought it was desirable that I should have a professional licence, and an Instrument Rating. I found the written examinations particularly difficult because it was so many years since I had gone into the theory of it all. Very good for me I don't doubt, but extremely hard work too. In those days, the written exams consisted mainly of short written answers, unlike the more modern multi-choice questions. I made the tactical error of completing both my basic 'navigation' group of exams and the technical group of exams in the same week. As a result by Friday afternoon I was totally mentally drained. I could have been mugged on the way home and I probably wouldn't have realised it.

During my four and a half years at the CAA I established a reputation for being one of the few people prepared to make a decision. I have usually taken the view that it is better to make a decision even if it turns out to have been not the best possible one, than to make no decision at all. With some notable exceptions, a large proportion of the staff of the CAA seemed to be only too keen to pass on any problem to someone else for a decision. If the RAF had taught me nothing else, at least they had taught me to assess a situation myself and then decide what to do about it. The rule of common sense seemed to cover most situations. Certainly, after I left the CAA I kept getting phone calls saying 'Go back Rufus, all is forgiven!'

For the last couple of years that I was with the CAA, I also used to work in the evening at the Piccadilly Hotel. There was an organisation there run by Monique Agazarian which provided flight simulator training for people living or working in London. I used to carry out any ground training the customers needed and I found that this helped to keep me up to date too. Monique was an extraordinary and delightful lady. She had learnt to fly during the early stages of the war, at her own expense, and then she had joined the Air Transport Auxiliary. She used to fly RAF aircraft – mainly single-seat fighters – from the factories to the front-line airfields. She was the only lady I knew who had not only flown more Marks of Spitfire than I had, but she had also flown more types of piston engine fighters. Her personal 'pilot's notes' which she showed me had an extra line 'Check Lipstick' inserted in the 'after landing checks' for every aircraft type that she flew. She had had a fabulous life in aviation, and used to carry out pleasure flights from Croydon and later, from Heathrow, in a De Havilland Rapide, until she was so pregnant that she was unable to get full movement of the controls.

Usually, when carrying out inspection visits at flying schools I used to go on my own, but occasionally another guy from the office would come with me. On one particular occasion I was due to go to Humberside to inspect a school and the head of my section decided that he would come with me. Most of the CAA travel by car on such visits, but since I got an allowance to keep myself in current flying practice, I considered that it would be much more appropriate to fly. On this occasion, I drove out to White Waltham where I collected a Cherokee 180 and flew over to Blackbushe to collect my boss. He was ready and waiting, and got in. I restarted the engine, taxied out, completed my checks, and when cleared, started my take-off run. Since it was a very hazy day I had put on my sunglasses to try and reduce the glare. After about 100 yards of my take-off run, I closed the throttle and told the Tower that I was aborting my take off. I explained to my passenger that I was on the wrong runway. I should have been on Runway 08 but I was on Runway 16.

'They don't have a Runway 16,' my passenger answered.

I back tracked, somewhat mystified, and lined up on the runway again. Sure enough it was Runway 16. I removed my sunglasses to look at my equally puzzled passenger and I put them back in their case. Re-examining the compass showed that we were, as we thought, on Runway 08. So I replaced my sunglasses and at once the compass swung to a heading of 16. That particular aircraft has the compass mounted in the instrument panel and I had put the case for my sunglasses on the coaming, out of the way. There was evidently a very strong magnetic field in the case which was causing the compass to give massive errors, so I put the case in my coat pocket on the back seat, well out of the way, and we continued with our flight to Humberside. Later I worked out that, with the error in the compass, we would have stood a very good chance of flying smack over the top of Heathrow. It would not have looked too good for two members of the CAA to infringe the London Control Zone. They say the devil looks after his own! However we had an uneventful flight except when we passed RAF Coltishall. Three Tornado aircraft were having a dogfight over the airfield, when we got there. So we joined in. I found that a Cherokee 180 will out-turn a Tornado but won't out climb it!

On another occasion when I was due to visit an airfield 'somewhere in the Midlands', I booked an aircraft from White Waltham as usual. I arrived at the airfield just before nine o'clock together with one of the clerical officers from the section who was going to help with the inspection. I duly contacted the duty instructor and introduced myself. He checked the board and confirmed that the aircraft was allotted and, so far as he could tell, was full of fuel. He then rather surprised me by asking when I last flew one of their aircraft.

'About four months ago,' I replied.

'Oh, then, you will need a dual check out before you go,' he said.

'OK,' I replied, 'who does that, you?'

He said that, yes he would be doing the check out and so I suggested that we went off as soon as I had been to the toilet. When I returned to the operations room, there was the duty instructor, bright red in the face.

'I'm awfully sorry, sir,' he said. 'I didn't realise who you were.'

I realised that he had had a king-sized flea in his ear from the owner and managing director while I had been out of the room, so I looked straight at him and said: 'Don't ever apologise for doing your job correctly. If your club rules say I should have a check out then that is what should happen. If I can't pass a check out, that's my problem. As you say, you didn't realise who I am so you were doing your job correctly.'

My clerical officer was having great difficulty maintaining a semblance of a straight face at the suggestion that a CAA Delegated Examiner and Type Rating Examiner would need to be checked out but, as I explained, if a guy is doing the job he is detailed to do then I have no right to complain just because I am a member of the CAA, and anyhow it would not have delayed us by much.

Just before I was due to retire, yet again – this time from the CAA – I was offered a job in Bournemouth as CFI of one of the schools there. I took the job, but with the advantage of hindsight this was a bad mistake. I should have waited until I had completed five years with the CAA and so qualified for a pension, and additionally, the management of the school didn't seem to approve of the fact that I tried to instil some discipline into the place and after a year we parted. This time I made a good move. I went to Southend-on-Sea where I look over as CFI of an up and coming school. They wanted to expand and to start doing instructor courses, instrument ratings and CPL training. We all worked well together and it was a very happy outfit. I bought a flat in Westcliffe-on-Sea so that I could become a fortnightly commuter, and I was able to help them build the school up into a thriving organisation with a small air taxi side as well. I have a few interesting memories of particular incidents of my time as chief instructor of these two schools which have managed to stick in my memory.

Bournemouth

Shortly after I arrived at Bournemouth, we leased an Aztec from its owner. I was asked to go up to Coventry to collect it and was told that it was due for a routine 50-hour check. Normally if there are no snags, it takes about four hours to complete. We preferred to do this inspection ourselves as we were naturally interested in knowing as much about the aircraft as possible. It is just as well that we did. It was in unbelievably bad condition. I have never seen an aircraft with so much wrong with it. If I had known about some of the faults, I would never have even considered flying it down from Coventry. For example, there was a heavy-duty brake on one side and a standard brake on the other. One engine was fitted with a 24-volt fuel pump and the other with a 12-volt pump (it was a 12-volt aircraft). All four fuel tanks were leaking and when removed were found to be beyond repair, and so it went on and on. Eventually we came to the conclusion that it was better to do an annual inspection on the aircraft. It was several weeks before we got it back on line and it cost the poor owner about as much as the aircraft was worth; but at least it had now got a large number of new bits on it and, as you would expect after such an extensive, not to say expensive, overhaul it proved to be very reliable and never once let me down.

We were contacted one day by a guy who wanted to hire our Aztec to take some friends to Le Mans for the race. This was no problem, but he was told that he would have to be checked out first. He came down to Bournemouth and seemed a bit disgruntled at the suggestion of having to do a check out at all, since he was a professional pilot and type rated on the Aztec. In due course we got airborne and although his handling was a bit on the crude side there was nothing dangerous until we got back to the airfield. On the first circuit, when we turned down wind, he went to lower the undercarriage at 160 knots – the limit is 150 – and I prepared to over-ride him. He noticed the speed OK, and commented that he was a bit fast. I relaxed. He then proceeded to take hold of both propeller levers and feather both engines. That really did slow us down. I woke up quickly, knocked his hand off the propeller levers, closed both throttles and unfeathered both engines. Fortunately, they both picked up OK, although by then we had lost about 400 of the 800 feet we had previously had. I handed control back to him. The landing was nothing to write home about so I allowed him to carry out a touch and go. That was my mistake. The next circuit was at least as untidy as the previous one and the landing was even worse. This time I instructed him to stay on the ground. As we taxied in I informed him that I was not prepared to let him hire our aircraft as I was not satisfied with his flying. You have never heard such language! Who the hell did I think I was to say he was unfit? He didn't accept that it had been a proper test. He was a professional pilot. He was rated on the Aztec anyhow. And so it went on and on. The outcome was that he didn't use our aircraft to go to Le Mans but at least he didn't get the opportunity to break it either.

On another occasion, I was asked to take a customer up to Doncaster in the Aztec. My plan was to let down at RAF Finningley and then go below the weather to Doncaster. In the event I took a co-pilot with me and we set off on what we expected to be a routine flight. Approaching RAF Finningley, I checked up on their weather. They were giving 250-foot cloud base and 1,000-metres visibility. This I decided was inadequate for a low-level run to Doncaster so I asked them if they would accept me as a weather diversion. After a bit of thought they informed me that OC Operations had declined to accept me and I should divert to East Midlands. This seemed to be no problem but a bit of a nuisance having to drive back to Doncaster. However, my guardian angel must have been airborne that day. I had only been en route to East Midlands Airport for about one minute when a voice came up on the radio: 'Finningley Approach, this is helicopter G—. I have just come from East Midlands. They have less than 20-metres visibility and are not allowing any take offs or landings and they are not allowing aircraft to taxi.'

'In that case G-BAVL, we will accept you for diversion,' they replied, 'turn and steer 150 degrees for Finningley.' Eventually, they gave me a PAR (Precision Approach Radar) and we finally broke cloud at 250 feet with rapidly decreasing visibility. Our passenger's car arrived shortly after we landed, having been sent over from Doncaster, and we agreed to pick him up the next afternoon from East Midlands Airport. The weather was worse the next day, however, and we had to contact the passenger and get him to return to RAF Finningley. We were in continuous cloud and rain almost all the way back to Bournemouth but shortly after passing Ibsley VOR, we came out of the side of the frontal system and were able to complete a visual recovery into Bournemouth.

Somehow during the first six months at Bournemouth, through what must have been gross carelessness, I managed to give myself a hernia, but the doctors organised a quick visit to hospital where it was stitched together again and a few days later I was back at work. I didn't fly until I felt fully recovered but I was able to get all the paperwork up to date and even get ahead of the game in part.

Southend on Sea

One day, about a year after I moved to Southend, I was asked to provide an aircraft to carry a photographer, so that Air UK, a locally based airline, could get some pictures of one of their Viscount aircraft. The cameraman contacted me and we prepared our Aztec with the side window and the centre row of seats removed. An extended safety harness was fitted so that there was no possibility of the cameraman falling out of the aircraft and a small cargo net was also fitted so that his equipment could all be restrained. Since the requirement was for me to formate in front of the Viscount's wing. I would be unable to maintain an adequate lookout and watch the wing of the Viscount at the same time, so I insisted on a fully qualified co-pilot who would be responsible for the lookout and for taking control if avoiding action was needed. The Viscount captain wanted to give me a long set of instructions on formation flying but when he found that I had spent a number of years flying fighter aircraft and teaching people how to fly in close formation, he accepted that I was possibly competent to fly near his aircraft. I can't say I blame him for being over-cautious as he would not have been able to dodge if I made a complete horlicks of it. I took off first and we climbed to height – around 6,000 feet. We were allotted three flight levels on the local airway entirely to ourselves and we were able to manoeuvre freely in that box. This made life much easier for both of us and in addition, our lookout was being duplicated by London Control by means of their radar. The weather was one of those glorious spring days with towering cumulus, a brilliant blue sky, bright sunshine and unlimited visibility. As a result the newly painted Viscount posed very prettily against some superb cloudscape backgrounds, while I developed a crick in the neck looking at the aircraft behind me. My poor co-pilot hardly saw the Viscount at all as he was following his instructions and keeping a good visual lookout.

After some 20 minutes, the photographer finished his rolls of film and we agreed with the Viscount pilot to call it a day. We descended rapidly to warmer flight conditions and landed back at Southend, followed by the Viscount. A couple of weeks later I got a large packet through the post. It contained a magnificent picture of a Viscount against a background which was half white cumulus and half Essex countryside. It was hung in pride of place in the school.

On air-taxi trips, I normally used one of our two Aztecs. It was an eminently suitable aircraft, but it is getting a bit out-dated now. On one occasion I had been over to Jersey to pick up an Air UK crew which had run out of duty hours. There was not much traffic about and London Control cleared me direct to Southend from a position well short of Midhurst. It was a lovely calm evening so I lowered the nose and allowed the speed to build up to just short of the limiting permitted speed and we were able to hold this right into the circuit at Southend. Here I managed to lose speed fairly rapidly and flew a tight circuit and landing. As I rolled down the runway, Air Traffic called me and said, 'G-OESX landed at 21.59 hours. Take the next exit left to the apron.'

I acknowledged the instructions and turned to the Air UK captain who was sitting in the other front seat.

'That's saved the company a bit of money,' I said, 'the landing fees go up to astronomical figures at 22.00 hours.'

'Ah!' he replied, 'I wondered why you were in such a hurry!'

It's nice when things work out for you.

One of our frequent freight loads was to carry day-old chicks to Ostende in Belgium. I was amazed to find that it was possible to get 5,500 live birds into an Aztec and still leave room for the pilot. The noise was deafening and the dust and smell a bit unattractive but it was normally only a 20-minute flight. I always tried to get the lowest level I could on my Air Traffic Clearance and usually I could go at 1,500 feet. I don't know if a greater altitude would bother the chicks but there seemed little point in not taking the kindest option. On one occasion when I went to pay my landing fee at Ostende, the controller told me that there was no need to tell him that I was carrying live chickens as he could hear them on the radio every time I spoke to him. Incidentally there is no truth in the rumour that we had to bang and shout to make them flap their wings before landing so that we were within the maximum landing weight.

Another Southend incident, which I was remembering recently, was a rather unusual night landing. My boss, Abigail, was flying in our Beech Duchess (a light twin-engine aircraft used for training). She had been doing some multi-engine conversion training combined with a bit of night flying with one of our students. They had been airborne for about an hour, when I was telephoned by Air Traffic Control and told that Abigail had been on the radio to say that she could not get the undercarriage to lock down. I was asked if I would like to go on to the airfield to have a look at it and naturally I accepted the offer. The Air Traffic Land-Rover picked me up and took me out to where the aircraft proceeded to over-fly at about 200 feet. Since it was a very black night, in spite of the mini search-light on the roof of the Land-Rover, I was unable to see anything of the aircraft other than its navigation lights. I called the Tower on the vehicle's radio and asked them if she could over-fly the apron, with all the flood lights set on full power. This was arranged, and again she flew past. This time the aircraft was clearly visible and I noticed that the main wheels were fully down and the nose wheel was fully up. Returning indoors, I called the aircraft on the company's radio frequency and spoke to the pilots. I checked to see that they had done all the normal things, like using the emergency system and selecting 'down' with both positive and negative 'G' applied.

As I expected, all the routine drills had been completed and it was evident that she would have to land with the nose wheel retracted. The question now was: should she land on the grass or the runway, and should she land with the main wheels up or down. I decided that the greatest chance of making sure that there would be no personal injury, would be to land with the main wheels down, on the runway, with both engines feathered and all the electrics and fuel turned off. I therefore spent some 15 minutes briefing the crew on exactly how they should do this. Who would do the flying; when they would shut each engine down; what speeds they should fly at and how much flap they should use. When they had absorbed all this advice and agreed with my plan, I told them to climb to a safe height and run through a dress rehearsal of what they were going to do, using touch drills, to see if there were any problems that I hadn't noticed or thought about. While this was going on, I briefed the fire section on our plans. I showed them another identical aircraft, and was able to indicate where the doors were and how they opened, how the harness releases worked and where the important switches were. And they too had a practice.

Some 15 minutes later (having cleared it with Air Traffic), I waited in a car at the beginning of the runway. Abigail did an excellent job of the landing and the aircraft passed me like a silent owl, with both engines feathered and both the propellers horizontal. The touchdown was gentle and when the nose could no longer be held off the ground, all the lights were switched off by the student and the aircraft slid along the runway on two wheels and a nose cone, coming to a halt some 15 yards past the point where the fire engines were waiting. Within a further 15 seconds of the aircraft coming to rest, the crash crew had arrived and two large firemen had opened the doors and picked up the seat occupants and carried them well clear of the aircraft. Damage to the aircraft seemed minimal and as soon as removal had been author-ised by the Inspectorate of Aircraft Accidents, we towed the aircraft back to the hangar. In the morning, an inspection revealed that the cause of the incident had been the nose wheel door, which had over run on its retraction and there was no possible way it could have been lowered. It was well and truly jammed. Using brute force and a crowbar, we removed the door and down came the wheel. Repairs consisted of fitting new doors to the nose wheel bay, making a fibre glass repair to the nose cone and straightening the bulkhead forward of the nose wheel, which was slightly buckled. Neither propeller had touched the ground so there was no further damage and the aircraft was soon back in service. The luck was definitely on our side that night. Normally, to land a multi-engine, propeller-driven aircraft at night with one wheel up would cause extensive damage to the aircraft. Our planning and rehearsals paid off with nil damage to the occupants and minimal damage to the aircraft. Almost the 'perfect' accident!

The Piper Malibou is a pretty hot ship for a piston engine aeroplane. Although only a single-engine aircraft, it seems to have just about everything important duplicated. I was asked one day to carry out an Air Test, for the initial issue of a Certificate of Airworthiness, on one which had just been imported from the USA. I was delighted to oblige. The aircraft was filled with fuel – all nine hours of it – and then the aircraft was loaded with ballast to bring it up to its maximum permitted take-off weight. Armed with the Flight Test Schedule, I took off with one of our company engineers on what we anticipated would be a routine flight. That was a bad mistake. There is no such thing in aviation as a routine flight. Although the aircraft was nearly new and had recently been flown over the Atlantic from the United States, things definitely did not go as expected. The first hiccup occurred during the maximum rate climb when it is essential that I fly the aircraft very accurately and write down the performance figures every 30 seconds so that we can draw a performance graph later. Suddenly red lights appeared all over the place. Looking to see what the captions read, I found that the alternator had failed and the battery was carrying the load. Out with the Flight Manual and I confirmed the correct drill. The standby alternator came on line correctly as a result and then I was able to bring all the circuits back into use. Meanwhile we continued with the climb. Eventually that part of the flight test was completed and we levelled out for the next tests. That's when the engine decided to quit. Again I ran through the drills and determined that there was nothing wrongly set and so, remembering that I had changed to another fuel tank a short while earlier, I put the high pressure pump on and sure enough, after a short pause, the engine picked up again and I was able to cancel the distress call that I had made to RAF Wattisham. I concluded that the engine failure was due to an airlock in the fuel system, which had been drained earlier in the day for some reason. Anyhow we were back in business again and so I continued with the Test Schedule. When I came to the timing of the undercarriage operation, all the red lights came on again. This time we had a complete hydraulic failure. Once more I told Wattisham about the problem. I decided now that enough was enough, it was time to go home as the aircraft was definitely trying to tell me something. I tried to descend, but here I found a problem. With the engine throttled back to the minimum turbine inlet temperature, and the aircraft flown at its limiting air speed, I found I only had 100 to 200 feet per minute descent. It was going to take for ever to get down from 9,500 feet. So I climbed to lose speed and selected undercarriage down on the emergency free-fall system. It worked as it should and the gear locked down. Now I could come down at the undercarriage limiting speed which is almost as high as the airframe limiting air speed and this gave us a respectable rate of descent. Next problem was what threshold speed to use for the landing? We only have short runways at Southend and there was very little wind. The over-run area is most unattractive as it is up a ramp and on to the electrified railway line.

Normally an aircraft of this type is landed at about 1.3 times its stalling speed. I had determined the stalling speed without flaps earlier and so I knew that it was 100 knots.

Even I could work out that sort of sum, but somehow 130 knots seemed a heck of a lot of speed with only a short runway and without the advantage of aerodynamic drag from the flaps which, of course, was unobtainable. So I settled for 1.2 times the stall speed. The wind was nice and calm and I didn't anticipate any handling problems. When the time came, I managed to hit 121 knots at the threshold, which I thought was pretty near and I found the handling was acceptable but delicate, to say the least. I definitely would not like to try and land that aircraft any slower without flaps, when it is at its at gross weight. We certainly settled on to the runway very early and there was almost no 'float'. As soon as I got the nose down I was able to use the brakes right away, and we managed to stop without any great difficulty. Altogether it was an 'interesting' flight which I somehow felt that the aircraft was not very keen to complete.

It was at about this time that there was an amusing but expensive incident at Southend Airport. The locally based Viscount aircraft were used for freight runs during the night to various destinations, returning in the small hours of the morning. On the night in question one of them had been on its usual route and when the time came for it to return, all the routine radio calls were made and the lights of the aircraft were seen on the final approach. The aircraft slowed to a stop on the runway and then nothing much seemed to happen. There were no radio messages and when called by the Air Traffic Controller, there was no reply. After a few minutes, the Air Traffic Land-Rover was dispatched to see what was going on. When the driver got there he was amazed to see the four-engine aircraft squatting on the runway on its belly with all four propellers twisted into knots and the undercarriage still fully retracted. He went to the aircraft and found the door unlocked so he entered to confirm the safety of the crew. He was even more amazed when he found that the aircraft was totally deserted. So he reported back to the Air Traffic Controller and in due course the recovery teams removed the aircraft. It was some days before the crew were found. I would love to have been a fly on the wall when they gave their explanation to their boss but, alas, I was excluded from that conversation.

The great storm of October 1987 had quite a marked effect on the environment of Southend. I was lucky, I managed to miss the worst of it by being at home in Plymouth when it struck. I can't say I am sorry to have missed it as by all reports it was very frightening. A few humorous and some not so humorous stories have come out of the gale.

One of our engineers at Southend was living in a caravan parked at the back of our hangar. He woke up to hear this eerie howling noise and being a guy of great loyalty, he got out of his nice warm bed at about half past one in the morning. He got dressed and then drove over to the other side of the airfield to make sure that all our aircraft were all right and to ensure that they had as many concrete blocks as possible tied on to them in an effort to anchor them to the ground. When he got there, he spent some time shifting every block he could find that was not already in use, and he then tied our aircraft down with at least five blocks each. The aircraft were parked facing into wind and the control locks were in place plus an additional lock on the rudders. While he was doing this he heard a yell and saw another of the ground crew who had been caught by the wind and bundled off his feet, and who could not even slow himself down, let alone stop. He was getting close so our engineer, at great personal risk lassoed him as he came past and managed to stop him being rolled clean across the apron.

Our buildings got off pretty lightly. The club house was relatively undamaged, just aerials blown off, and our hangar had two of the sheets of cladding twisted off. Others did not do so well. There was a blister hangar on the far side of the airfield and quite early on, this subsided on top of all the aircraft inside. Most of them were written off as a result. Of the aircraft parked outside, near the blister hangar, a PA28 ended up in a tree and an Auster took off and crashed about 100 yards away. There was sundry other damage from flying objects but most of it was repairable. A DC9 airliner parked on the main apron was blown 30 yards backwards although it had the parking brakes on and was properly chocked. One guy, who had a privately owned Cessna 150, heard the wind howling and he too got up to go and see that his aircraft was OK. He drove on to the airfield and stopped his nice new Volvo about 20 yards in front of his aircraft. He then got out and as he walked round the back of the car, there was an almighty bang and his aircraft landed upside down on top of his nice new Volvo. As he later said, 'if only I had stayed in bed, the aircraft would still have been a write off but at least my car would have escaped!'

My top floor flat down on the seafront didn't do so well. The wind came across the river estuary at about 100 mph and then had to accelerate up the slope of the seafront gardens. When it reached the buildings it then had to accelerate again to get over them and through the gaps between the buildings. In the case of my block of flats, it is estimated that the wind between the buildings got up to well over 140 mph and managed to suck several hundred of the bricks out of the wall. It also took all the chimneys and all the slates off the roof and so, when I returned on Monday, I found that my flat was both air conditioned and water cooled. The whole of the roof had gone and the rain came in. My front door had been broken into by other occupants of the block of flats in an effort to reduce the amount of water pouring down to the flats below. There was a lot of damage inside the flat and I had to evacuate permanently. I managed to buy a flat in Westcliffe – naturally at a time when house prices had just about reached their peak – and I stayed there until I moved back to Exeter, a few years later. It was astonishing how many buildings in Southend managed to have broken windows facing the seafront, which they got their insurance companies to replace with new double-glazed units.

About a week after the storm, I was asked to fly a party of forestry commission guys to assess the damage to the Kent and Essex woods. It was unbelievable how many trees had been blown down. In the woods a lot of it was due to a 'domino' effect where the first tree fell down under the effect of the wind and it knocked the next two down which knocked the next four down and so on right across the wood. It was sad to see so much damage but within 20 years, it will be impossible to see from the air. And 20 years is nothing to the lifetime of a forest.

Not long before I left Southend, I had to complete one of my routine six-monthly Base Checks. This is a test of my flying skills to ensure that I am able to deal with all the 'normal' emergencies. The test started with the aircraft over at Stansted, and there were four of us in the Aztec, the other three were the Type Rating Examiner who was doing the Base Check, an Instrument Rating Examiner who was also renewing my Instrument Rating and another pilot who had done his renewal tests on the way to Stansted. Anyhow, the weather forecast was definitely within limits although it was overcast and a bit windy. I took off and naturally had the 'mandatory' engine failure shortly after getting airborne. I dealt with this and after finishing the 'general handling' part of the test, I set off with the 'failed' engine shut down, back to Southend where we were intending to carry out a single-engine NDB approach and landing. The track to Southend was about 140 degrees and I steered 155 to allow for the fairly strong south-westerly wind. The instruments did not seem to be giving the expected readings and so I had to obtain a number of fixes. We seemed to be moving to my left very rapidly and I ended up steering 180 (due south) to get to Southend. There was obviously an abnormally strong wind and when I reached the Southend beacon, I needed to make a course reversal. Normally this would involve a 30-degree turn, flown for one minute and a standard rate turn on to the opposite heading with about one minute to run back to the beacon. In view of the wind, I went southbound for three minutes instead of one minute and then started my turn. During the turn I passed over the beacon. I quickly turned on to the outbound heading of the Instrument Approach Procedure. This track should have been maintained for three minutes, descending and then followed by a right turn to come back to the airfield, descending to the Minimum Descent Height on the way back. I decided that I would go out-bound for only one minute (and I explained to the examiners why). I then turned and established the correct track back to the airfield. I decided not to lower the undercarriage until I saw something I recognised as the single-engine performance with the wheels down and four occupants is not very good (to say the least). I continued homing back to the airfield for eleven minutes before I saw anything I recognised. (It felt like much longer but that is what the watch said.) I then lowered the wheels and eventually I selected one only third flap, to improve the handling without significantly increasing the drag. I crossed the beginning of the runway, landed and stopped without needing to use the brakes at all, before the first intersection. As I turned off, I asked the Tower what the wind strength was.

'It was about 60 knots when you landed, but has been gusting up to 75 knots,' was the answer. It felt like it! (75 knots is 86 mph.) Normally I wouldn't dream of flying in such a wind but it was about 20 knots at Stansted when we took off and had been about the same when we took off from Southend earlier. Also, for what it's worth, the wind at height is normally quite a bit stronger than the wind on the surface. The upper winds that day must have been between 70 and 90 knots, unlike the forecast which only talked about 25–30 knots of wind.

Flying around the north Essex area one day I noticed what I thought was a big bonfire. From a distance it looked as though it was in the garden of a large house just north of the town of Tiptree. My flight took me a bit nearer to the smoke and it was then I realised that the smoke did not come from a bonfire but from a large wooden hut. Flames were coming from the door and windows at one end and, as I watched I saw a couple of people jump out of a window at the other end. The hedge of trees was starting to burn too, and so I called the Air Traffic Control at Southend and asked them to contact the fire brigade in Tiptree and tell them about this building which was on fire. They did this and within a very few minutes we were able to watch the fire engine come out of town towards 'my' fire. They overshot the entrance but stopped, reversed and drove in. By this time, other aircraft in the local area who had heard my call to Southend were all converging on 'my' fire so I departed. I didn't want to get involved in a swarm of aircraft orbiting the fun and games on the ground with none of the pilots looking out for each other. It's too easy to have a collision and that can ruin your day.

Exeter
The Exeter Flying Club was asked periodically to provide an item for local airshows and displays. The normal programme which we put on consisted of four Cessna 150 trainers which carried out a formation take off, followed by three or four flypasts in different formations ending with a run in echelon from which each aircraft peeled off into a landing. At least, three of them landed. In the fourth aircraft I climbed as hard as I could – which is not very rapidly in a Cessna 150. As the last of the other three aircraft landed, I would go into an aerobatic sequence. I was cleared down to a minimum height of 200 feet above the ground and so, at the 'top' of the manoeuvres, I was about 1,000 feet above ground. My final aerobatic consisted

of a loop with a half roll off the top of the loop. As I rolled, I pulled the mixture fully back to the 'cut off' position and held the nose high until the engine stopped completely. I then carried out a 'forced landing' with the engine stopped, coming to rest, neatly parked in the line of aircraft in front of the crowd. It is one of those flashy manoeuvres which looks very exciting but is actually quite easy (especially after practising that morning, and telling the other pilots where to leave the gap in the line).

I have always considered that display aerobatic pilots can be split into two groups. The professional display pilots who are in continuous practice and who do two or three shows and at least half a dozen practices every week, and the 'amateur' display pilot, such as myself, who has to work up to standard before each and every display. After each show, the amateur display pilot ought to land shaking, from the excess of adrenalin in his system, because if he doesn't, then he is getting over-confident and that is the day before he kills himself. (There are no minor accidents in low-level aerobatics.) Sometimes it would be half an hour before I settled down to normality after a display.

I was doing a show at Exeter one afternoon as part of the RAF Association Air Day. We had done all the usual things. The flypasts were quite steady, the other aircraft had landed and parked as briefed, my aerobatics had gone well and the final forced landing worked out perfectly. As usual, I rolled to a halt exactly in the gap in the aircraft line and I climbed out. As I walked back to club house I noticed that I was not shaking. When I got to the club house, several people remarked on the display and how much they had enjoyed it.

'I'm glad you enjoyed it,' I said, 'because you will never see another one. I have stopped doing them.'

I didn't know I was going to stop then, but during the short walk back to the club house, I decided that since I was not full of adrenalin I was getting over-confident, so I determined to take my own advice and stop doing low-level aerobatic displays. And I have never done another one. I think my wife, Olive, was quite pleased although she had never tried to discourage me from doing these displays.

It is quite easy to lose something small. Medium-size objects can usually be kept to hand and big things are very difficult to lose. Yet I know of one pilot flying a Britannia who managed, not only to 'lose' Exeter but he even managed to 'lose' Devon. He was due to fly into Exeter to pick up some freight. The normal flight plans arrived, he called on the radio. He gave his position as being some 20 miles to the east of the airfield and he was cleared to carry out a straight-in approach on Runway 26. Some minutes later he announced that he was 'visual' and shortly after he reported on 'finals.' He was cleared to land and our eyes turned to the east to watch him land. There was total silence and no sign of a large four-engine transport aircraft. Air Traffic asked him for a position report.

'I'm just coming over the hedge,' he replied.

'Not here you aren't,' said Air Traffic. 'Go around, I say again go around.'

He acknowledged and climbed straight ahead to 3,000 feet. Still no sound or sight of him. After a significant delay there was a rather embarrassed voice on the radio.

'I'm visual with the airfield. Am I still clear for a straight-in approach?'

He was cleared again and he landed, this time at Exeter. The earlier 'approach'? That had evidently been at the naval airfield at Merryfield in Somerset. It is surprising how many pilots have landed or tried to land at the 'wrong' aerodrome. I was flying a Chipmunk from St Mawgan in Cornwall one day. As I approached to land I was told that I was 'Number 2 to an aircraft on finals. Looking hard, I was unable to spot any aircraft on finals. Looking a bit further afield, I spotted an aircraft on short finals to the disused

172

airfield at St Eval, a few miles north of St Mawgan. I called the Tower, 'St Mawgan, is the aircraft ahead of me a Viscount aircraft?' I asked.

The reply was unhelpful, 'Continue your approach DYF 65, the other aircraft is on finals.'

'Wilco,' I replied, 'but if the aircraft ahead is a Viscount, he is about to land at St Eval.'

There was no reply, but the aircraft I was watching turned hard right and then hard left to line up with the runway at St Mawgan, where it landed. The world contains two sorts of pilots. Those who have landed or tried to land at the 'wrong' airfield, and those who will.

Some four or five years ago, I was asked to carry out a twin-engine rating course for a guy who, up to then, had only flown single-engine aircraft. He was allowed to use the family's company aircraft, a Cessna 340, and so we started his first flight. As usual, this consisted mainly of 'effect of controls' to enable him to see and feel how the aircraft reacted to the alternative control inputs. We got around to examining the effect on the aircraft of lowering the undercarriage. Making sure that we were well within the limiting speeds for this, I instructed him to select undercarriage 'down'. This he did and we noted the slight trim change, the airframe buffet, and the increase in drag. He then asked, 'Shouldn't there be three green lights, sir?'

'Yes,' I replied, 'what do we have?'

Two greens and a red,' was the answer. So we tried a re-selection. And another. And another. But all to no avail. The right leg refused to lock down. We tried positive and negative 'G'. We tried yawing the aircraft, we tried combinations of methods. All to no avail. We tried the emergency lowering system but still no third green light.

'We seem to have a problem,' I told him. 'We will return to base and try again when we get there.'

So he flew the aircraft back to Exeter, keeping the speed well below the permitted undercarriage-down speeds. On arrival, we told the Tower about the problem and following half a dozen more selections, we carried out an overfly of the field so that the people on the ground could look at it and let me know its exact position. The Tower told us that the leg seemed to be just about fully down. So at least we knew that it was not in the fully 'up' position. We made a few more attempts to lower it and also asked the Tower to see if a friend of mine was on the field, because he used to operate a Cessna 340 and might know some trick which I didn't know about. A couple of minutes later, he was on the radio. We had already tried all the options he suggested, so it seemed that we were committed to landing with that leg unlocked.

I briefed the student on the three possible results: the leg might collapse and cause us to swing to the right; the leg might not collapse but might not lock, or the leg might lock on touchdown when the weight came on it. Just for once I found that I had a student who really was paying attention to what I said. I told him that I had decided to shut down the right-hand engine to minimise damage to the propeller and engine if the leg did collapse under us, so first I made a practice approach to get the feel of it, as it was some while since I had landed that type of aircraft on two engines, let alone on one. When the moment of truth arrived, I did a very careful, gentle touchdown and to our great pleasure, not to mention relief, the leg locked down. You can't beat a jolly good anti-climax in these circumstances! So we restarted the shutdown engine and taxied back to the hangar to get it fixed. It turned out to only be an incorrectly adjusted micro switch but as far as I was concerned a leg without its associated green light on is an unsafe leg. I'm a great believer that 'Cowardice prolongs Active Life'.

18 August 1992
A strange subtitle but a date which is engraved in my memory. Nothing much to do with flying this time. I had

decided that since the ravages of old age cannot be kept at bay for ever, it was time I went to see the medics with a view to having a routine minor operation which comes to all male pilots. The doctors agreed and the surgical consultant made the necessary arrangements. A few days before the operation I was asked to go and have a couple of routine tests and when I turned up they took my blood pressure, took a 'specimen' and took a blood sample to ensure that they had the right mix available in case they needed it. Two days later I got a phone call asking me to come back as they had found a problem and had cancelled the operation. When I get there, the consultant apologised but told me that there was a problem with my blood and he had been advised not to operate until the cause had been identified. So he gave me a string of additional tests which he wanted done and I spent a few days visiting all the necessary departments. They took x-rays, blood samples, an ultra-sound scan, bone marrow samples and various guys poked, prodded and pummelled me in all directions. Then it went quiet. After nearly a week in which I was imagining all sorts of problems from beri-beri to death-watch beetle, I got another phone call asking me to go in. So the next morning Thursday 13 August, I duly presented myself at the consulting room. The consultant arrived just before nine o'clock and took me upstairs and sat me down.

'Right Mr Heald,' he said. 'We have found the problem and I have some good news and I have some bad news. I'll start with the bad news. I'm afraid I have to tell you that you have cancer. We have found a tumour on your right kidney. The good news is that I have booked the operating theatre for next Tuesday. I intend to remove your right kidney and the tumour.' He then sent me for a test to ensure that the left kidney was working OK. It was and I went back to work at the flying club. My mind was not on the flying for once. Indeed, I knocked off early and went home. I did not have a very pleasant weekend, and I can truthfully say that it was probably one of the worst I have ever had. On Tuesday 18 August I reported to the Nuffield Hospital and that evening I was wheeled off on a trolley with a smile on my face after the pre-med injection had taken effect.

The following morning I woke up, to find myself in a plumber's nightmare of pipes. There were plastic pipes going in and out of all sorts of places and I found that I was extremely sore. Not surprising really since I now had a 16-inch scar running across my body just below the equator. The surgeon called to see me later and said that he was delighted with the way it had all gone. Everything had come out cleanly. The tumour had measured $8 \times 10 \times 10$ centimetres, but was totally self contained and had not got into my system. He didn't anticipate any more trouble from it. He pointed out how lucky I was. It was causing no pain or even inconvenience, yet in six months I would have been in a lot of constant pain and in 12 months he would not have wasted time operating. It was quite restful lying there. I didn't need to move for anything and lots of nice young ladies came to visit me. All good things come to an end and on Sunday, Olive came and collected me and took me home. I took life very gently for a few days and slowly got back into my stride. I was quite surprised when the surgeon said that he could do the original operation a fortnight after the first one. Anyhow, that went off as expected and a few days later I went off on a bit of convalescence in Wales. When I got back I gradually built up my strength (what strength?) and then went back to work. I had been flying for quite a while when I got a call from the dreaded CAA asking why I was flying as I was grounded medically. I pointed out that I was not grounded and I had a valid medical. They suggested that I should have told them about the operations, but I pointed out that I had not been incapacitated by illness for more than 28 days. When I asked why they thought I should be grounded, they told me that I had cancer and how did I think they would feel if I developed a secondary and was suddenly incapacitated and dived into the ground killing myself and my student. My reply was fairly restrained in the circumstances: 'B— how you would feel. How do you think I would feel?' I replied. And then added, 'Firstly, I don't have cancer, not now. Secondly, secondary tumours don't "suddenly incapacitate" you and even if they did, my student would simply come back to Exeter, land and roll me out.' The doctor seemed to think that the student might not be able to do that but I was able to point out that the CAA had already given all my students a professional licence so they ought to be happy that he could land a Cessna training aircraft. Anyhow they insisted that I had to be grounded for three months from the date of the operation. That took me to 18 November but I persuaded them that the 16th was a better date as it was a Monday. They agreed, so for the next six or seven days I could only do ground training. Then I was back to three sorties a day to catch up. So I will always remember Tuesday 18 August 1992.

I may add that I have had no further problems in that department and long may it last. The really pleasant news, though, was that I had joined PPP Health Insurance less than a year before the operations and they paid for me to be 'done' in the Nuffield Hospital with no delay. The devil was still looking after his own.

8

Third Retirement: 1993–96

During the major recession of the early nineties, it seemed a good moment to retire from full-time instructing and so I left the Exeter Flying Club and looked around for enjoyable and gainful activity. I didn't have long to wait. Within a few days, word had got out and I had a phone call from Plymouth School of Flying asking if I could go down and discuss the possibility of doing some specialised instructing for them. The guy who had been doing their instructor training had medical problems, and so they were looking for someone to take over where he had left off. I explained that I was not looking for anything full time, but I would be happy to help them out when they had a customer. We soon came to an agreement over remuneration etc. and I now go down there when they send for me. It makes a break for my wife when I am there and I usually stay with my son who lives in Ivybridge, just outside Plymouth.

This was obviously going to leave me with more spare time than I wanted, so I contacted a number of schools in the United States, Australia and New Zealand to see if they wanted a UK representative, and I also circulated all the instructor training schools in the UK to let them know that I was available as a locum if they needed a back up. My Examiner Authority was still valid and this enabled me to carry out a number of flight tests on various people and additionally I was nominated as training captain for several mini air-taxi/pleasure flight companies throughout the south-west.

At the request of Heather Atkinson, the editor of *European Flight Training News*, a tabloid-size paper published monthly, I wrote a number of articles on flying training, concentrating on the continuation training of pilots after they had got their licences. These turned out to be very popular and I had a number of complimentary telephone calls. I have since written some 30 articles for the paper and now that Heather has sold the title, I am establishing a similar relationship with the new editor.

I was called in a few months ago to advise a group on the licensing and registering of a light amphibian. It made an interesting diversion from the norm and I also found that the members of the group required some flying refresher training. One of them had let his PPL lapse and he needed to do some 15 flying hours and some re-examinations in order to reactivate his licence and another of them had let his Instructor Rating lapse. He needed to refresh the whole of the Instructor Rating Syllabus and this made a pleasant break from the norm. Quite a number of other guys have been in louch with me to see if, and when, I can do some advanced training for them and, to top it all, I have been persuaded to carry out instructor training at four different schools.

December 1993 was an interesting month. The flight crew of all airlines within the UK were required to have completed a course of training in Crew Recourse Management and Human Performance and Limitations by the end of the year. They all suddenly cottoned on to this fact and, apart from the larger companies, they had to find a trainer. I am one of the very few freelance approved trainers for this course and I was very much in demand by all the small air taxi and charter companies in southern England. Altogether I was called in by 17 different air lines who between them operated some 35 different aircraft types. So I had to mug up on their specific aircraft types the night before the training. My first day off that month was 23 December, and I needed it. I was getting a bit punch drunk. I was lucky, in that I have flown over 350 different types of aircraft, so I was able to relate to the vast majority of the ones which I had to refer to during the training. One month like that, per year, is quite enough. The only flying I did during that period was as a passenger en route to the next training session.

One of the advantages of retirement is that you can usually plan your holidays well ahead. Last year, my daughter decided to get married in Mombasa, so this gave me the excuse for me and my brother-in-law to take our wives and go on a safari type holiday in Kenya, ending up in Mombasa just before the wedding. The flight out was very uncomfortable and the food was poor to say the least but the weather on arrival at Nairobi was excellent. We night stopped in a rather scruffy hotel and the next day we were collected by the driver of a Nissan minibus who stayed with us for the whole of the safari. Fortunately his command of English was a lot better than my command of Swahili, which is limited to a hundred words or so and a few 'useful phrases'. The country was just as it had been in 1947 when I was last there. Indeed I think some of the pot holes in the roads are the same ones. We stayed at five different game lodges and there is no doubt that it is a photographer's heaven. The light is good and the variety of wild life is unbelievable. I managed to take about 450 photographs during the week, using a new and very expensive camera which I got a couple of weeks before we set off. The safari ended up in Mombasa and the hotel was excellent. The wedding and the subsequent reception went off without a hitch – more photographs of course, and a couple of days later we flew back, first from Mombasa to Nairobi and then from Nairobi to Heathrow. I had a slightly better seat on the return trip but the food was just as plastic. Having waited the mandatory 45 minutes for our luggage to appear, we just managed to catch the coach back to sunny Devon, tired, sunburnt and broke – but happy.

This year my wife and I went to Southern Ireland. The natives were just as friendly but the wild game was less evident. This was more than compensated for by the fact that the Guinness was excellent – I couldn't fault it. We flew by British Airways to Cork this time and then hired a car for a week. There is no doubt that, out of season, the only way to travel in Southern Ireland is by minor road and without an itinerary. We found excellent hospitality everywhere we went and we both enjoyed the break immensely.

In 1983, a couple of years after I had joined the Civil Aviation Authority, the medics found a small irregularity in my six monthly ECG. So I was invited to go for a run on the treadmill to confirm that there was no serious problem. This I completed successfully – to my great relief – and the doctors confirmed that the irregularity vanished under slight stress and didn't return. I suppose that that was one of the penalties of living on the fat of the land in London. Anyhow, in 1996, I got another invitation to go to the CAA and have a second gallop on their treadmill. This is a routine test which they ask all professional pilots to undergo when they reach the magic age of 70. Several of my friends had failed the test when they went, so I was more than a little worried. I persuaded my daughter to lend me her exercise bicycle and I carried out numerous rides on that. In due course the great day arrived and I presented myself at Gatwick. I had night stopped with my mother in Guildford and I had allowed two hours for what is normally a one-hour journey. As a result I arrived reasonably unstressed and offered my body to the doctors. To cut a long story short, I found it quite easy and after I had recovered and changed into clean clothing, I went back to the consultant's office. 'That was excellent,' he said. 'I dug out the test we did in 1983 and I think this one is even better. We won't ask you to come back for another run for five years.' You have no idea what a weight this was off my mind. For some reason or other, the CAA seems to think that age is important so far as the health of a professional pilot is concerned. That is absolute rubbish. Some guys of 60 or 70 are a lot fitter than others who are only 50 and I have no doubt that, provided the medical staff are prepared to give me a Class I medical certificate, then I am 'fit' to operate as a professional pilot. Nevertheless, there is a faction within the CAA Flight Crew Licensing Department which tries to limit a pilot's licence privileges on the basis of his age, rather than on his ability to fly the aircraft safely and skilfully.

When I was working in the CAA in the 1980s I often thought that pilots who had been trained in the United States tended to be given a raw deal. Some of the American schools are excellent but others were not nearly so good. Indeed many at the lower end of the market tended to pay lip service to the training, sign the guy off and ship him back to the UK. The trouble was that the majority of those pilots going to America for their training went there to save money. They studied the advertisements in the UK Aviation Press and selected the cheapest. That is exactly what they got. If they had said, 'Let's go to the worst school we can find,' they would have probably searched the UK Aviation Press and selected the cheapest. 'Nuff said?

Anyhow I thought that it might be an idea to set myself up as the UK representative of some reputable schools so I opened a dialogue with several schools which did not have representatives in this country. In the fullness of time I was appointed as the UK representative of one in New Jersey. But they were fairly expensive and got very few customers – so they abandoned the idea of recruiting customers in the UK. I also took on representation of a school in Florida. They were quite a good school and were owned and managed by a guy from the UK. He claimed to be ex-Royal Navy. I sent him lots of customers but when the time came for him to forward my small commission, he had a variety of weak excuses as to why he could not send it yet. I am still waiting and don't expect to get it. I do not recommend his school any more. Then I tried one in Arizona. This is based in Prescott and the chief instructor is a guy from Dartmouth in Devon. They tend to be a bit expensive because they don't bother too much about the minimum hours for training pilots. They believe in minimum standards and I agree with them that these are more important than minimum hours. So they tend to take longer than some of the other schools and so some customers feel they are being overcharged. These are the pilots who are primarily interested in price not in quality. I also tried representing a Canadian school. They had a good product and good prices but a policy of advertising which was unlikely to attract many customers. As a result they didn't get many and so they too have decided not to recruit customers in Europe. Unfortunately, there are a vast number of rip-off merchants in aviation, and guys who are keen to see how much they can get out of aviation, rather than seeing how much they can put into it. Meanwhile I continue to give free advice to anyone who wants to know about the overseas pilot training set-up. I hope that I will save some of them from the more excessive rip-off merchants.

Now that I am gradually taking life rather easier I still seem to have no time to myself. How the hell I ever managed to have time for a full-time job defeats me. Recently, I have been asked to write articles for one of the leading aviation magazines; I have a couple of firms of solicitors asking me to advise them in the capacity of expert witness; I write odd bits for the Aviator's Network on the Internet, and I still seem to get a number of guys wanting me to train them as flying instructors or professional pilots. Plus a few who just want me to polish up their flying. I suppose that I must be a workaholic because I still enjoy it. I still manage to get a great deal of pleasure by passing on to the next generation some of the skills and knowledge which I have amassed over the last fifty plus years. I keep telling them that they won't have time to make all the mistakes themselves but it somehow doesn't seem to stop them! I have no doubt that I will continue to pass on what I can. After all I have had a fabulous career, flying some of the most wonderful military aircraft and then training my replacements. I just hope that some of the guys who follow will be able to look back eventually and say that they have had as good a life.